Dear Reader,

Can you solve this riddle: What's three thousand years old but still as new as tomorrow's sunrise?

It's a hard question, especially in our world when new software released today makes yesterday's version instantly obsolete.

So, what's old and new at the same time? Not computer programs or things, only ideas, and the books that bring those ideas into our minds and hearts.

The Bible is that kind of book. Its stories tell about friendship, love of God and each other, about fear and hatred and war. For three thousand years its stories have excited and comforted people of many faiths. Today, as always, people find in the Bible a direction—a way to live.

You'll get a glimpse of the Bible's old and new treasures in this book. Enjoy it and then, I hope, go on to learn more.

Chaya

The Kids' Catalog of Bible Treasures

The Kids' Catalog of

Bible Treasures

Written and Illustrated by

Chaya M. Burstein

The Jewish Publication Society
Philadelphia
1999 / 5760

The Jewish Publication Society
1930 Chestnut Street
Philadelphia, PA 19103-4599
Design and composition by Eliz. Anne O'Donnell
Manufactured in the United States of America

99 00 01 02 03 04 05 06 07 08 09 10 9 8 7 6 5 4 3 2 1

Library of Congress Cataloging-in-Publication Data

Burstein, Chaya M.
    The kid's catalog of Bible treasures / written and illustrated by Chaya M.
Burstein. — 1st ed.
        p.   cm.
    Includes index.
    Summary: Presents text, cartoons, crafts, maps, portraits of Biblical figures,
games and related activities as resources for reading and understanding the
Bible, particularly the part known as the Old Testament.
    ISBN 0-8276-0667-2
    1. Bible. O.T.—Juvenile literature. 2. Bibles stories, English—O.T. [1. Bible.
O.T. 2. Bible stories—O.T. 3. Judaism—Customs and practices.] I. Title.
BS539.B87 1999
221.9'5—DC21   99-11591
                                                                        CIP

Sources

Tanakh, the Holy Scriptures, published by The Jewish Publication Society has
been my Bible source throughout the writing of this book. On page 58 I adapted
two *aggadot*, "legends," from *Legends of the Bible* by Louis Ginzberg, published
by The Jewish Publication Society. The illustrations on page 73 were drawn from
reconstructed models of Bible instruments at the Haifa Museum in Haifa, Israel.
The Rest Is Commentary by Nahum N. Glatzer, published by Beacon Press was
the source for my adaptation of the Oral Torah on page 85. *Saul Raskin,
Paintings and Drawings* contains the original drawing of Oif'n Pripitchek on page
89. The story "How to Live Happily Ever After" on page 97 was adapted from
Legends of Judea and Samaria by Zev Vilnay, published by The Jewish
Publication Society. *Folktales of Israel*, edited by Dov Noy and published by the
University of Chicago Press is the source of the story "The She Goats of
Shebrezin" on page 104. And finally the diagram for Telling about Tells on page
111 was drawn from an exhibit at the museum of Kibbutz Sasa in Israel, with fur-
ther explanation by my friend and kibbutz member Eshel Spiro.

*Our rabbis and teachers tell us
that the Torah was handed on from Moses
in a continuing chain.*

*This book is for my grandchildren,
**Raizel, Naomi, Avishai,
Rivka,** and **Jacob,**
who are links in that chain.*

Acknowledgments

Many thanks to Rabbi David Sperling who kindly reviewed and commented on the text of this book. Thanks also to Bruce Black, Children's Book Editor, who patiently encouraged and guided me as the writing proceeded; to Dr. Ellen Frankel, Editor-in-Chief, who provided a well-informed, critical overview; to Dov Goobich and Ed Toben who contributed their photo-taking skills generously and repeatedly as this book developed; to Sim Goobich who scanned the text with her educator's eye; to Anne O'Donnell whose creative design enhanced the content; and to copyeditors Tara Ann McFadden and Sydelle Zove. My warmest thanks to my husband Mordy who happily explored the mountains, deserts, and cities of Israel with me until the Bible landscapes came alive for both of us.

Contents

Mini-Dictionary

aggadah (ah gah DAH): a legend based on the stories of the Bible. Also refers to the stories of the Talmud.

B.C.E. and **C.E.**: from the words "Before the Common Era." The Jewish way of designating the centuries before and after the birth of Jesus.

First Temple: built in Jerusalem by King Solomon around the year 950 B.C.E. and destroyed in the year 586 B.C.E.

Gemarah (geh MAHR ah): the thoughts and deliberations of the ancient rabbis who studied Torah and Mishnah. Two versions were written, one around the year 400 C.E., the other about 100 years later. The combination of the Mishnah and the Gemarah together make up the Talmud.

messiah: originally a Hebrew word meaning "anointed one," usually a king, chosen by God. Many Jews believe that God will someday send a messiah to redeem the world. Christians believe that Jesus Christ is the Messiah.

midrash (MID rahsh): a lesson, often in story form, derived from the stories of the Bible.

Mishnah (MISH nah): the teachings of the ancient rabbis as written down in the year 200 C.E. Also called the Oral Torah since for centuries it had been passed down from generation to generation by word of mouth.

Second Temple: construction began in the year 538 B.C.E. when the Jews returned to Jerusalem from exile in Babylonia. Destroyed by the Romans in the year 70 C.E. All that remains today is a portion of its Western Wall, built by Herod.

sofer (SO fer): a person who copies, by hand, the words of the Torah. Tradition requires that this scribe use black ink and a feather pen, or quill, and that the letters be written on parchment, a material made from the skins of goats or sheep.

stele (STEE lee): carved stone used in ancient times to create sign posts at important buildings or sites.

Tanakh (tah NAKH): the name for the three sections of the Bible—Torah (the Five Books of Moses), Nevi'im (the Prophets), and Ketuvim (the Writings). The word Tanakh is an acronym formed by putting together the first lettrs of the Hebrew words for each of the three parts.

tell: an ancient hill formed over the centuries by the building up and destruction of a succession of settlements.

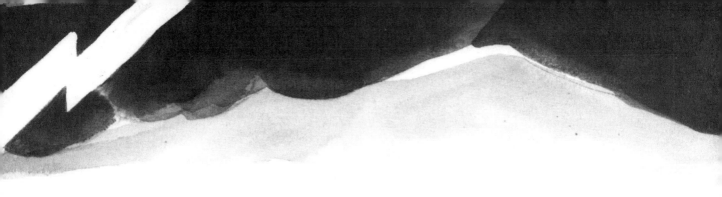

Introduction

Thunder shook the mountain, shofars blared, and smoke and flames filled the desert sky. The crowd of Israelites was too frightened to move. They closed their eyes, covered their ears, and shivered. Moses, their leader, was gone. He had climbed the dark mountain to speak to God. First he had dragged them out of Egypt, and then he had left them alone in this thundering desert. They didn't know if he'd ever come back.

When Moses finally stepped out of the smoke and clouds, the Israelites cried with relief. He was carrying the Ten Commandments, God's gift to the Jewish people. And he also brought the laws of the Bible, which God had taught him on Mount Sinai. Now, finally, the people felt safe. God and Moses and the Bible would lead them through every danger and bring them to the Promised Land.

Sounds good—but that's not exactly what happened. The Israelites did accept the Ten Commandments. But they soon started whining. They were hungry, or homesick for Egypt, or their feet hurt, or they needed a drink, or they were scared. A lot of the time they disobeyed the Bible's rules. Moses and God had to scold and punish the Israelites. And then they had to feed and comfort them to keep them going. Finally, after a hard, forty year walk, the people of Israel reached their land.

That walk through the desert happened about thirty-three hundred years ago. And the Bible has been part of Jewish life ever since. Like the Israelites in the desert, Jews today sometimes complain about the laws and customs that have grown from the Bible. But reading and understanding the Bible gives many people a feeling of purpose and meaning in their lives. It gives others a sense of God's role in the world. The Bible is here with us today as it was in the days of Moses.

How does the Bible connect to you? Turn the page and jump into the life of a Bible kid. Follow the Bible connection from Adam and Eve all the way to the twenty-first century.

1 Flying above the Land of the Bible

Here's how to reach the land of the Bible. Roll your imagination back almost 4,000 years. Then zoom east 6,000 miles from the east coast of the United States. It's a long trip, but luckily for you there's an easy make-believe way to go. A flying Space-Time-Travel-Effectuation-Vehicle (STEV) has just landed in your backyard. All the lights are flashing. All systems are "GO." Climb in.

Go Go Go with Your STEV

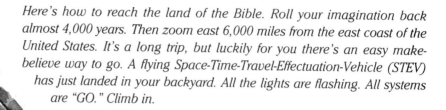

"Wel-come-a-board," says a creaky door-ish voice. "I-am-your-Space-Time-Tra-vel-E-ffec-tu-a-tion Ve-hi-cle. You-may-call-me-STEV. Fas-ten-your-seat-belt. Set-the-time-dial. Re-com-mend-set-ting-for-pre-A-bra-ham-ic-Ca-naan-nine-teen-hun-dred-B.-C.-E. Set-lo-ca-tor-but-ton-for-Ca-naan-and-press-START."

Okay! A make believe trip doesn't scare you at all. You follow instructions. The STEV shivers and begins to hum. Through the view-er screen you see the backyard barbecue and the tomato plants drop away. You're going up! Your stomach feels like it's dropping away too. The roofs of houses and criss-crossing streets slip by underneath you. After a few seconds there are green fields and twisting rivers. Then white sand, and suddenly you're over a gray ocean.

You'll be flying east across the Atlantic Ocean, Europe, and the Mediterranean Sea. That could take forever. "Hey STEV, is there an in-flight movie?" you ask. The STEV's hum turns into indignant grunts that sound like, "Short-at-ten-tion-span-gen-e-ra-tion!" You notice a red button marked "hyper-speed." You push it, and with a "va-room" the STEV zooms forward.

Gray ocean, . . . more gray ocean, . . . more gray ocean, . . . and then patches of brown. More ocean, more land, . . . and with a click the STEV lurches out of hyper-speed and slows down. Blue-green water sparkles below. This must be the Mediterranean Sea. It's dotted with boats. Some have tall masts and brightly colored sails. Some have shiny oars sticking out of their sides, moving up and down like the legs of a big bug. Of course, you remember, people are pushing those oars. Poor people! There were no motors in Bible times. People or the wind or animals were the power that moved things.

Cruising over Canaan

A strip of white sand flashes by. Beyond the sand you see green fields. Red lights flash on the information panel above the viewer screen. A message appears. It reads, "You have reached your destination. You are cruising eastward above the Land of Canaan in the year 1900 B.C.E. In the future Canaan will be known as the Promised Land or the Land of Israel. For further information see the Five Books of Moses, known in Hebrew as the Torah."

"Wow!" you exclaim. "This is the Land of the Bible. The Land of Milk and Honey!"

text continued on p. 6

B.C.E.??????

Question: When did the events in the Bible happen?

Answer: In B.C.E.

Question: Huh?

Answer: B.C.E. means Before the Common Era. Some people say the Christian Era since it begins with the birth of Jesus, who started Christianity. The first year of the Common Era was 1 C.E. We live almost 2,000 years later.

Question: So when was B.C.E.?

Answer: B.C.E. is the way we count years before the Common Era. The numbers grow larger and larger as we count back into history. Here's how it looks on a time line.

B.C.E. ⟵ ⟶ C.E.

| about 1800 Abraham and Sarah came to Canaan | about 1300 Moses brought the Hebrew tribes to Israel | 586 First Temple destroyed. Jews exiled to Babylonia | 70 Romans destroyed Second Temple | 1492 Jews expelled from Spain | 1948 State of Israel established | ? Your birthday! |

A STEV View of Canaan

In the Bible, God promised a wonderful land to the Jewish people:

"The Lord your God brings you into a good land, a land of brooks of water, of fountains and springs that rise from valleys and hills; a land of wheat and barley, and vines and fig trees and pomegranates; a land of olive trees and honey. A land where you shall eat bread without scarceness. You shall not lack anything in it. A land whose stones are iron and out of whose hills you may dig copper."

DEUTERONOMY 8:7–9

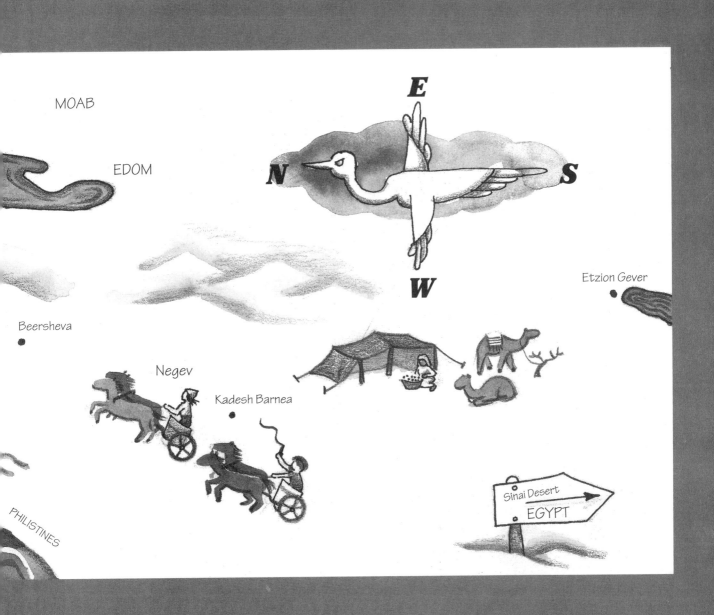

The STEV is cruising over a flat, green plain striped with narrow, brown fields. An ox is slowly dragging a wooden plow through the earth. A man walks behind it guiding the plow. Small brown houses are scattered across the plain. Gray-green olive trees and wide-branched fig trees are growing around them. On the ground in front of one house, a woman is sitting and turning a large round stone on top of another stone.

Before you can push "Information" to ask what she's doing, you've passed the green plain and you're rising over bumpy hills. Tall trees are growing between gray rocks. A herd of black goats is climbing the rocks.

And a boy with a headband and shaggy black hair is following them. "Hi!" you yell and wave. He doesn't wave back. Maybe you and the STEV are invisible.

Now there are just trees and rocks. Oh wait—there's a trail in the valley between the hills. A line of donkeys loaded with large baskets is moving along the trail. A skinny, old man is riding in front and people carrying spears and bows are walking alongside. They must be afraid of wild animals or of robbers. Just past a turn in the trail you suddenly see a group of men hiding behind rocks. Their bowstrings are pulled tight. Their arrows are aimed at the trail. Robbers? "STEV!" you yell, "We have to warn those people with the donkeys!" But the STEV sails on and in seconds the people and donkeys are gone.

The Big City and the Desert

There's a town coming up. You can see the smoke of cooking fires hanging over the trees. Square, stone houses spread over the hills. It's a big city with people and wagons crowding the streets. Orchards of fig, almond, and olive trees cover the hillsides below the houses and grapevines climb over the stone walls. Nice place, you think and press

"Information." The name "Jerusalem" flashes on the panel. Oh sure, you know all about Jerusalem. One day this city will be the capital of Israel. The Jews will build their Temple here. But not yet.

After Jerusalem the mountains slope down. The land turns a pale, oatmealish color. There are very few trees or houses, just some black tents and more goats. Off to your right, to the south, there are more pale hills. "Is this all desert?" you wonder. Push "Information" and ask about southern Canaan. The panel reports, "Southern region known as the Negev gets very little rain. Wandering tribes live in the Negev. Further south are the Sinai Desert and Egypt."

"I know that," you say, feeling very smart. "In a few hundred years, Moses will bring the Jews out of Egypt and up through the Sinai Desert to Israel."

"Ouch!" Your head hits the roof as the STEV bumps up and down. You've passed the hills and now you're flying over a huge, steaming, gray lake. The STEV is bouncing on heat waves rising from the water. Quick, push "Information." The words "Dead Sea" flash on the panel. "A body of water too thick with salt and other chemicals to support fish or other living things. The lowest spot on the earth's surface." STEV's creaky voice breaks in. "Cau-tion! You-are-now-leav-ing-Ca-naan-and-en-ter-ing-Mo-ab. Please-ad-just-Lo-ca-tor-dial-or-you-will-end-up-in-Chi-na."

"Very funny," you say. You quickly adjust the Locator dial to read "circle around the Land of Canaan." The STEV turns north following a squiggly river. "The Jordan River," explains "Information." It also explains that the town underneath you with thick walls and swaying date palm trees is called Jericho. To your right, east of the Jordan River, the hills of Moab have become the hills of Ammon. To the west a line of mountains runs up through Canaan like a rocky backbone.

"No person ever drowned in the Dead Sea," said the Israelites. The water of the Dead Sea is so heavy with minerals that it's easy to float on the surface. If you can't swim, come and test this theory.

You See Some Family

Here comes another lake. It's much smaller than the Dead Sea and not at all dead. It's dotted with fishing boats and surrounded by villages and palm trees. Push "Information." The words "Lake Kinneret, also known as the Sea of Galilee," appear on the panel. "A fresh water lake that feeds the Jordan River." A wide road runs beside the lake and then cuts across the country to the Mediterranean shore. You see another long caravan moving along this road. People, donkeys, sheep, oxen, and goats. There's something special about them. You feel a tug, as if you know them. That's silly. How could you know anyone who lived almost 4,000 years ago? But you push down on the Altitude lever and the STEV drops to the tops of the palm trees. Bouncing along on two donkeys at the head of the caravan are a broad-shouldered man with a bushy, white beard and a gray-haired, dark-eyed woman. "I know them!" you shout. "That woman looks just like my Aunt Sarah!" Push the "Information" button. The words flash on the panel, "Abram and Sarai, whose names were later changed by God to Abraham and Sarah. They were the patriarch and matriarch of the Jewish people."

"They're my relatives!" you yell. You ask for more information. The panel reports, "Abraham of Ur will make a covenant or agreement with God. God will promise to make a great people grow from Abraham and Sarah, and God will give them the land of Canaan. See the Bible for further information."

"I knew they were my relatives. I have to go down and say 'hi.' Maybe I can give them a hint about what will happen in the future." You push the Altitude lever as far down as it will go. The STEV begins to buck up and down. A siren yowls like a tomcat. Red lights flash on the panel. In huge red letters you see the message, "CAUTION! STEV NOT PRO-GRAMMED TO LAND IN ALTERNATE TIME ZONES! CAUTION!"

"Okay, okay, don't get so upset," you say and push up the Altitude lever. "Aunt Sarah will never forgive me for not saying hello."

The STEV zooms up and out of the Jordan Valley and turns west over the cool, wooded mountains of northern Canaan. Here and there between the trees you see sparkling streams and foaming waterfalls. Great hiking and picnicking country.

Bible Landscapes

You can explore Bible landscapes without flying a STEV. Take an ordinary jet to Israel. Then take an ordinary bus to Neot Kedumin in the hills near Jerusalem. It's a Biblical park where hills and valleys have been shaped and plants, trees, and flowers of the Bible have been planted. Wander from the steamy jungles of the Jordan River to the cool olive groves of the Galilee between breakfast and lunch. There are no lions or bears . . . yet. Until you can get to Neot Kedumim, take a look at these photos of Bible landscapes. PHOTOS COURTESY OF DOV GUBITCH

Trouble in a Temple

But then—too soon—the Mediterranean Sea is ahead. You've made a full circle. Just before you reach the sea you notice smoke rising from a hill to the north. You push the Altitude lever down a little to get closer. A fire is blazing on a platform in a square courtyard, and people are dancing around a tall, black boulder. Other people are pulling a small, struggling boy toward the platform. What's happening? Push "Information." "Canaanite temple" appears on the panel. You ask for more information. The STEV reports, "The Canaanite temple is a center for worship, dancing, and sacrifices to the gods. Children are sometimes burned on the altar as a gift or sacrifice to the fire god—Moloch."

With the whole world to choose from, why would God bring the Jewish people to the bare, tiny land of Israel where there is rocky soil and very little water? Some wise-guys explain that it's because Moses stuttered. When God asked Moses to which country he'd like to lead the Jews, Moses said, "Ca-Ca-Ca..."

"Done!" said God. "I'll give you Canaan." "Oh no!" thought Moses, "I meant to say Canada."

"Wait a minute!" you yell. "They're going to throw that kid into the fire! I can't let them do that!" You push down hard on the Altitude lever. STEV starts to bounce, red lights flash, and the siren yowls. Huge red letters fill the panel. "CAUTION! STEV NOT PROGRAMMED FOR LANDING IN ALTERNATE TIME ZONES. CONTROLS ARE NOW BECOMING AUTOMATIC!" The altitude lever sweeps up and the STEV shoots up. The temple, the fire, and the little boy are gone. You can see only the beach and the blue sea. "STEV, please go back. I have to save that boy!" No answer. Instead a new message flashes on the panel. "Round trip of Canaan is complete. Fuel running low. Returning to point of origin immediately."

The STEV tips, like a bicycle making a tight turn, and heads out over the sea. With a "va-room" it whips into hyper-speed. You feel so helpless. You couldn't help the caravan that was about to be robbed. And you couldn't help the Canaanite boy. Then you remember Abraham and Sarah, your ancestors. You saw them coming to Canaan. They believe in the God of the Hebrews so you hope they won't ever, ever have human sacrifices. They'll make things better in the Land of the Bible. You start feeling better . . . and that makes you hungry. You wonder if the STEV has an in-flight snack. Just then the panel lights up again. It announces, "STEV will now present our in-flight entertainment of the week." The viewer screen turns silver. Cool, you think and settle back to watch.

Just the Facts

"This week's entertainment consists of a map and data on the Land of Canaan in 1900 B.C.E. Some Biblical sites will also be shown. Please study the map as you read the display."

"Wait a minute," you yelp. "That's not entertainment! How about a Disney movie?" The STEV makes a snickering sound as a map flickers onto the panel. Beside the map you read the word "Data" and the following text:

"Canaan is a small country, about as big as the twentieth century American state of New Jersey. It has a mild climate with dry summers and rainy winters. Fertile farmland is found along the Mediterranean coast, the Jordan valley, and in the valleys that cross the country from east to west. A chain of wooded mountains runs north and south between the sea and the Jordan River. Most of the neighboring lands have less rain and more deserts. The rich towns of Canaan are often attacked and robbed by their hungrier neighbors. Wildlife includes

SO THAT'S WHERE IT COMES FROM

So That's Where It Comes From!
Names of the Land of the Bible

Canaan—name of the land before the tribes of Israel conquered it

Promised Land—an often-used name since God promised this land to Abraham and his descendants

Land of Milk and Honey—in the Bible, God described the land as fruitful and flowing with milk and honey

Land of Israel—after the tribes of Israel conquered Canaan, it became the Land of Israel

Judah (Judea) and Israel—after King Solomon died, the kingdom split into these two parts

Palestine—many Jews were driven out of Judea by the Romans who changed the country's name to Palestine, named after the long-gone Philistines

State of Israel—in 1948 C.E. the new Jewish state was founded in part of Palestine

*The stone cliffs along the Amud
stream in northern Israel are as full of
holes as Swiss cheese. Hundreds of
caves look down on the stream.
Orchards of fruit trees and ancient
water mills still line the banks.*

deer, bears, lions, jackals, porcupines, and boar. The first book of the
Bible tells us that much of Canaan and the surrounding areas are
promised by God to Abraham, Sarah, and their descendants."

The panel goes blank. Then a message in small print flashes on:
"This completes STEV's in-flight entertainment for the week. STEV, Inc. is
pleased to announce that you are entitled to one bonus flight to the destination of your choice. Details will be announced shortly."

"Yeessss!" you exclaim, "I'm ready when you are!"

The STEV lurches out of hyper-speed and coasts down. Gray ocean,
then a grid of roads, towns, houses . . . and there's your shopping center,
your school, your street! Hold onto your stomach. You're dropping fast.
The STEV hums, groans, rattles, and settles gently into your backyard,
right on top of the tomato plants. "STEV, get off!" you shriek. "My mother
will kill us both!" With an insulted burp the STEV lifts off and comes
down on the lawn. You climb out and turn to say goodbye, but the
Space-Time-Travel-Effectuation-vehicle is already humming away, barely
missing the TV antenna.

And now you're on your own. To find out more about the Bible, the
Promised Land, Abraham and Sarah, and all the rest, turn to Chapter
Two.

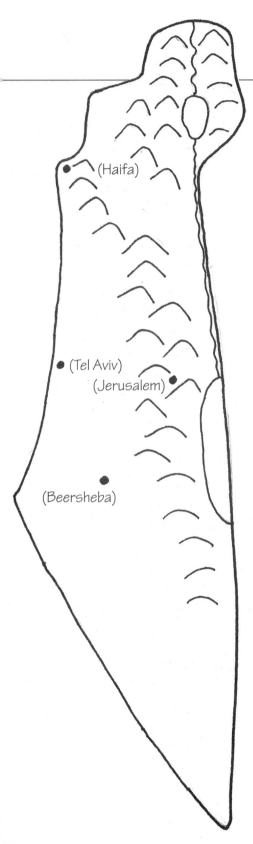

(Haifa)

(Tel Aviv)

(Jerusalem)

(Beersheba)

Bible Crafts: Make a Bread Dough Map of Israel (NOT for eating!)

To make the bread dough you will need:

> 1/2 cup of hot (not boiling) water
> 1/2 cup of salt
> 1$\frac{1}{3}$ cups of flour
> measuring cup
> bowl
> spoon for mixing

1. Add the salt to the hot water in the bowl. Stir well.
2. Add the flour. Mix well. Knead the mixture until the dough is smooth. If the mixture is too sticky to knead, add a tablespoon of flour.

To make the map you will need:

> sheet of baking parchment about 3$\frac{1}{2}$ inches by 10 inches
> cookie sheet larger than 3$\frac{1}{2}$ inches by 10 inches
> cardboard or other board larger then 3$\frac{1}{2}$ inches by 10 inches
> tape
> glue
> acrylic or watercolor paint and brush
> toothpicks
> paper for names

1. Trace the map outline from this page onto the baking parchment.
2. Place the baking parchment on the cookie sheet. Tape it at corners to hold it flat.

3. Press half of the bread dough inside the outline. Add bits of dough to build mountains. Dig away dough for the lakes and seas. You can use a pencil tip to shape mountains and seas.

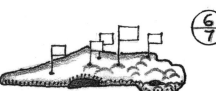

4. Make a hole with the toothpick at Haifa, Tel Aviv, Beersheba, and Jerusalem. Make a hole in the center for the flag of Israel.

5. Remove the tape. Bake in the oven at 250 degrees for one to two hours until the bread dough map is hard and dry.

6. When the map is cool, peel off the baking parchment, spread glue on the underside of the bread dough map, and glue it to the board.

7. Paint blue for the water, green for valleys, brown for the mountains . . . or whatever you choose. It's *your* map.

8. Write the city names and "Israel" on small pieces of paper. Glue them to the toothpicks and glue the toothpicks into the holes you made in #4.

Note: This is a simplified outline. With peace agreements, the outline of the map of the State of Israel may change.

2 The Greatest Book Ever Written

Thanks to STEV you know that the Land of the Bible (which used to be called Canaan) is a green, fruitful land on the shore of the Mediterranean Sea. Most of the stories in the Bible happened there. But the Bible doesn't begin with the story of the land and the people of Israel. It begins by describing how the whole world began.

Stories, Laws, and Lessons

People read Bible stories in different ways. Some believe that God gave the entire Bible to Moses, and every word in the Bible means exactly what it says. Other people add their own ideas and explanations to the words of the Bible. Either way, many believe that the Bible is the greatest book ever written. It tells exciting stories about heroes and bad guys. It tells about God's covenant (agreement) with Abraham and his descendants and about the kings and prophets of Israel.

Harsh tales of battles and killing are mixed with stories that teach us to be fair, honest, and kind with each other. And when we feel sad about the world because so many people are poor and sick or fighting wars, the Bible gives us hope that people will live together happily some day.

A printed Bible is a very fat book. It has three sections. The first section is called the Torah, or the Five Books of Moses. The second section is called Prophets (*Nevi'im*). The third is Writings (*Ketuvim*).

Tanakh is another name for the three sections of the Bible—in Hebrew תנ"ך. The name is formed from the first letter of the name of each section —

תורה	Torah (Five Books of Moses)
נביאים	*Nevi'im* (Prophets)
כתובים	*Ketuvim* (Writings)

This chapter tells some of the stories of the Five Books of Moses (the first section of the Tanakh) in pictures. In Chapters Three and Four you'll find out about Prophets and Writings.

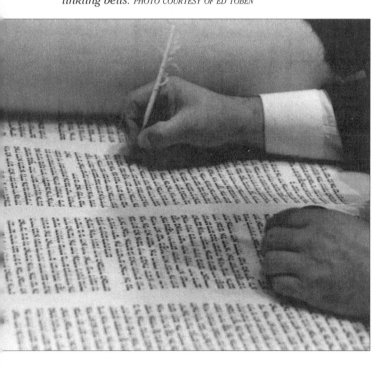

The Torah scroll in the synagogue contains the hand-written text of the Five Books of Moses. A sofer, or "scribe", carefully copies each word. He uses black ink and a feather quill, and writes on a piece of thin leather called parchment. The pieces of leather are sewed together into a long scroll. The scroll may be kept in a cloth wrapper or in a wooden container, which is decorated with painted or embroidered designs, precious stones, gold and silver chains, and tinkling bells. PHOTO COURTESY OF ED TOBEN

The Five Books of Moses

In the beginning there was a great, dark emptiness. Only the spirit of God moved in the emptiness. And God said, "Let there be light!" God divided the light from darkness. God called the light "day" and the darkness "night." There was evening and morning. The first day.

God divided the emptiness into an upper and lower part. God called the upper part "heaven." And there was evening and morning. The second day.

God gathered the waters under heaven and let dry land appear. "Let grass and trees and flowers grow," said God. There was evening and morning. The third day.

LET THERE BE STARS IN THE HEAVENS

Then God made the sun and the moon to rule over day and night. And there was evening and morning. The fourth day.

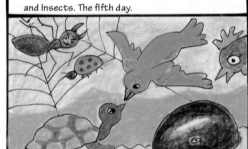

God created the fish and sea monsters, birds, and insects. The fifth day.

"Let there be cattle and large, wild animals and small, creeping animals," said God, "and I will make human beings to rule over all living things." God made a man and a woman and said to them, "Be fruitful and multiply." God saw that creation was good. And it was evening and morning. The sixth day.

On the seventh day God's work was finished. God blessed the seventh day and called it holy because on that day God rested from all work of creation.

LEAVE THE GARDEN OF EDEN!

Adam and Eve were the first man and woman. They lived in the Garden of Eden with animals, flowers, and trees around them. God said, "You may not eat the fruit of the tree of knowledge of good and evil." The serpent persuaded Eve to eat the forbidden fruit. She gave some to Adam. God sent them out of the Garden of Eden.

It was hard to find food and bear children out in the world. Adam and Eve had two sons called Cain and Abel. The boys fought and Cain killed Abel.

WHERE IS ABEL?

How should I know? Am I my brother's keeper?

Adam and Eve had many descendants. Most of them were cruel and violent. Only Noah and his family were good people.

God got disgusted with all the evil. God told Noah to build an ark and bring aboard his family and pairs of all living things.

Then God made rain fall for forty days and forty nights. The earth was covered with water. Noah and his ark filled with God's creatures floated on the water. They were the only living things left on earth.

THE RAINBOW IS MY SIGN. I WILL NEVER AGAIN MAKE A FLOOD TO DESTROY THE EARTH

After many days the water went down. Everyone climbed out of the ark and found a clean, empty world.

People kept doing wrong things. Noah's descendants began to build a city with a tower that would reach heaven.

We're almost up to heaven!

To stop them God made each builder speak a different language. They babbled at each other until they got angry. Then they threw away their tools and ran off. The great unfinished tower was called the Tower of Babel.

God spoke to Abram of the land of Ur.

GO TO THE LAND THAT I WILL SHOW YOU AND I WILL MAKE OF YOU A GREAT NATION.

Abram and his family went to the land of Canaan.

Sarai, Abram's wife, had no children. She gave her maid Hagar to Abram as a wife. Hagar bore Abram a son called Ishmael.

God spoke to Abram.

I WILL ESTABLISH MY COVENANT WITH YOU AND YOUR DESCENDANTS, TO GIVE YOU THE LAND OF CANAAN. AS A SIGN OF THE COVENANT YOU WILL CIRCUMCISE ALL YOUR MALES.

God said, "I will change your name to Abraham, father of many nations. Sarai will be called Sarah. She will bear a son to carry on the covenant."

Sarah laughed when she heard God's promise. She was 90 years old and Abraham was 100! She called the baby Isaac, which means "laughter."

Abraham's nephew Lot moved to Sodom, a town of thieves and murderers. God decided to destroy Sodom and its neighbor Gomorrah. God warned Lot and his family to escape.

Don't look back!

Lot's wife looked back and turned into a pillar of salt.

When Ishmael made fun of Isaac, Abraham sadly sent Hagar and Ishmael away. God made a well of water for them to drink in the desert.

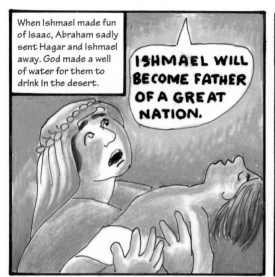

ISHMAEL WILL BECOME FATHER OF A GREAT NATION.

God decided to test Abraham. God told Abraham to sacrifice his son Isaac. Abraham took Isaac up to a mountaintop. Just as Abraham raised his knife over Isaac, God sent an angel to stop him. Abraham found a ram to sacrifice instead of Isaac.

Isaac and his wife Rebecca had twin sons. Esau, the older twin, became a hunter. Jacob, the younger, liked staying home. When Isaac grew blind and old he wanted to bless Esau. Jacob pretended to be Esau and Isaac blessed him instead. Then, afraid of Esau, Jacob ran away.

Bless me father, please

I'd better leave before Esau gets home

Years later Jacob came back with his wives, his many children and flocks of sheep and goats. On the way home he fought with an angel who gave him a new name—Israel, the one who struggles with God. Esau and Jacob made peace with each other.

Listen guys, in my dream you all bowed down to me.

Rachel, Leah, and their two handmaids, Bilhah and Zilpah, had twelve sons and a daughter with Jacob. Joseph was Jacob's favorite son. Jacob made a brightly colored coat for Joseph. The boy had many dreams. The dreams made Joseph's brothers angry and jealous.

They sold Joseph as a slave to merchants who were going to Egypt. Then they told their father that Joseph had been killed by a wild animal. Jacob cried bitterly.

Egypt will have seven years of good crops - and then seven hungry years.

In Egypt Joseph explained the dreams of the king of Egypt, the Pharaoh. Joseph became Pharaoh's advisor and soon ruled the whole land.

The seven dry years began. The wells dried up and the crops died in Egypt and Canaan. Joseph's brothers came to Egypt to buy food. They didn't recognize him. At first Joseph was mean and teased them. But later he revealed who he was and invited his whole family to come live in Egypt.

As years passed the numbers of Hebrews grew. Each of Jacob's sons became the father of a tribe. The new Pharaoh was afraid of them. He enslaved them. And he drowned all the Hebrew boy babies that he could find.

A Hebrew mother named Yokheved hid her baby boy in a basket beside the river. His sister Miriam guarded him until Pharaoh's daughter found him. The princess adopted the baby and called him Moses.

When Moses grew up he killed an Egyptian who was beating a Hebrew slave. Then he ran away to the desert. One day he saw a bush that burned and burned without burning up. God's voice spoke to him from the bush.

BRING MY PEOPLE OUT OF EGYPT! I WILL BRING YOU TO A LAND OF MILK AND HONEY

Moses and his brother Aaron went to the Pharaoh and begged him to let the Hebrews go.

NO WAY!

Then God sent ten terrible plagues to force Pharaoh to change his mind. God turned the water into blood and sent frogs, lice, and gnats. God caused the cattle to get sick, boils to grow on people, hail to fall, locusts to eat crops, and darkness to cover Egypt.

Worst of all was the tenth plague. It killed every first-born Egyptian child and animal in the land of Egypt. Only the Hebrews were spared.

At last Pharaoh let them go. The Hebrews quickly baked a flat bread called matzah and ran into the desert. God set a pillar of fire in the sky to guide the people at night. In the daytime they followed a cloud.

Pharaoh changed his mind. The Hebrews waited by the Red Sea and cried when they saw the Egyptians chasing them.

God sent a strong wind to push the water back. The Hebrews ran across the dry sea bed. Then the sea flooded back and drowned Pharaoh and his army.

Miriam and the other Hebrews sang and danced and thanked God for helping them.

Deep in the desert Moses and the Hebrews came to Mount Sinai. Clouds covered the mountaintop and horns blared. The frightened people waited while Moses went up into the clouds and thunder to speak to God.

God gave the Ten Commandments to Moses and taught him other laws for the Hebrews, the people of Israel.

When Moses came down after forty days he found that his people had made a calf of gold. They were singing and praying to it as though it was a god.

A golden calf ?!!

Angrily, Moses smashed the Ten Commandments.

God gave the people another chance. Moses went up to the mountaintop again. He brought down two new tablets of the Commandments. Then he read God's laws to the people. They brought silver and fine cloth and built the Mishkan, a portable Temple to worship God. Men of the tribe of Levi carried the Mishkan as the Hebrews walked on through the desert.

At the border of the Promised Land Moses sent in twelve spies. They came back with huge bunches of grapes. But ten of them gave a frightening report. It scared almost everyone.

It's a land of milk and honey.

It's a land that eats its own people.

Giants live there.

God grew angry at the people.

YOU ARE FRIGHTENED BECAUSE YOU DON'T TRUST ME. NOW YOU MUST LIVE IN THE DESERT FOR FORTY YEARS. AFTER THE DEATHS OF THOSE WHO WERE SLAVES, I WILL BRING THEIR CHILDREN INTO THE PROMISED LAND.

The Hebrews walked in the desert for forty years. They were often thirsty and tired. They had to fight many enemies.

Finally when Moses was one hundred and twenty years old he led his people to the Jordan River on the border of the Promised Land. Again Moses taught God's law to the twelve tribes of Israel.

Here are the laws of the Torah. Follow them carefully.

Moses' Great Last Lesson:
Remember your agreement with God. Fear and serve God. Love and protect the stranger. Don't ever forget that once you were strangers in the land of Egypt. Teach your children to obey God's laws. Help the needy. Remember and celebrate the holidays of Passover, Shavuot, and Sukkot. Observe the Shabbat. Appoint religious judges. And follow all of God's other laws. If you do these things you will be a holy people and God will bless you and your land. I have set before you this day life and good, and death and evil. Choose life. Love the Lord, your God. Walk in God's ways and keep God's commandments . . . and the Lord will bless you in the land to which you go. (Deuteronomy 30)

Moses chose Joshua to lead the people. Joshua was one of the spies who had not been afraid to fight for the Promised Land.

Moses' work was done. He climbed to the top of Mount Nebo and looked sadly across into the Promised Land. How he wished he could have touched its soil. And then Moses died.

For thirty days the Hebrew people mourned their great leader. Then Joshua commanded them, "Get ready! In three days we will cross the Jordan and take the land that God has promised to us."

Wise rabbis agreed that people may understand the Torah in different ways. They wrote, "As a hammer strikes many sparks, so does a single verse of Torah have many meanings."

THE TEN COMMANDMENTS

The Ten Commandments are shown on the doors of arks in modern synagogues. They are also often embroidered on the curtain of the ark or on the cover of the Torah scroll. *PHOTO COURTESY OF ED TOBEN*

1. I am the Lord, your God. You shall not worship any other god.

2. You shall not make statues or pictures of living things in order to pray to them.

3. Do not use My name, the name of God, to swear falsely.

4. Remember the Sabbath day and keep it holy. You, your family, servants, guests, and work animals may work for six days, but not on the seventh, because God made heaven and earth in six days and rested on the seventh.

5. Honor your father and mother.

6. You shall not kill anyone.

7. You shall not take another man's wife or another woman's husband.

8. You shall not steal.

9. You shall not lie about your neighbor.

10. You shall not want something that belongs to your neighbor.

3 About Judges, Kings, and Prophets

At the end of the last chapter we left the Hebrew tribes standing on a riverbank across from the Promised Land. They were frightened. Moses was gone. He had been a father and teacher to them for as long as they could remember. Without him they felt like orphans. God had promised to help them, but God seemed so far away. They couldn't see or hear or touch God. Would their new leader, Joshua, be smart enough and strong enough to help them win their new land? It was a scary time.

What happened to the Hebrew tribes next was both a blessing and a curse. They won the Land of Israel but often forgot God's laws. Here are some of the highlights of the story that's told in the Book of Prophets, the second section of the Tanakh.

SO THAT'S WHERE IT COMES FROM

So That's Where It Comes From!
The Bible's Seven Species

The Israelite tribes stood in the dry, rocky Sinai Desert and listened hungrily as God described the fruitful land to which they were being brought. It was a land of seven good things—wheat and barley and grapevines, fig trees and pomegranate trees, olive oil, and honey (often made of dates).

—DEUTERONOMY 8:7–8

Conquering the Promised Land

Joshua led the twelve tribes of Israel across the Jordan River. They set their tents outside the high walls of Jericho. The city gates were locked against them. As God commanded, for six days they walked around the walls carrying the Holy Ark. On the seventh day they blew their shofars and let out a great shout. The walls came tumbling down and the Israelites charged in and captured the city. After that many other Canaanite cities were conquered or surrendered. Then Joshua divided the land between the tribes. Each tribe settled in its own place to build homes and plant fields. And each tribe gave cities and pasture lands to the people of the tribe of Levi who were the priests and took care of the Holy Ark.

The Twelve Tribes of Israel
Genesis, Chapter 49

The tribes of Israel grew from the families of each of the sons of Jacob. Each tribe had a symbol which may have been carried before it during the forty-year walk through the desert. Synagogue arks or windows are often decorated with these symbols.

Fighting Judges

So far, so good. But new troubles were coming. Enemies like the Midianites, Canaanites, and Philistines came to attack one Hebrew tribe at a time. They would steal cattle and burn fields. Sometimes they would rob travelers on the road or snatch people away to be slaves. Strong leaders and fighters led each of the tribes. They were called judges. When a tribe was attacked, the judges often called on other Hebrew tribes to help them fight their enemies.

Deborah was a judge who liked to sit quietly under a tree and settle arguments between people. She hated fighting. But one day a huge Canaanite army with 900 iron chariots marched down to attack her tribes of Zebulon and Naftali. It was led by a cruel general called Yavin. Deborah had to fight. She and her general, Barak, led the army of Israelites up the steep sides of Mount Tabor. The Canaanite chariots rolled into the valley below and stopped beside the Kishon River. The Canaanite spearsmen, swordsmen, and archers sharpened their weapons and waved them threateningly. They were itching to fight.

Mount Tabor rises out of the Jezreel Valley like the crown of a giant's hat. An Arab village called Daburriya sits on its slope. Some people think the village was named after Deborah the judge. PHOTO COURTESY OF MORDY BURSTEIN

"Should we attack?" Barak asked.

"Wait," said Deborah. As they waited, black clouds filled the sky. A few drops fell. Then the drops became a flood of rain. The river rose over its banks. The valley became a swamp of gooey, gluey mud. Chariot wheels sank into the mud and couldn't budge. The horses and men in the valley slipped and skidded. Then Deborah yelled, "Charge!" The Israelites shot arrows into the tangled Canaanites and swept down. In a panic, the enemies dropped their weapons, left their chariots, and ran. The Israelites had won the battle!

Deborah went happily to sit under her tree and she sang a song of thanks to God. "Oh God," she

sang, "when You marched out the earth
shook and the heavens dripped."

As years passed, the Israelites began to feel at home in their
Promised Land. They got to know their neighbors. Some Israelites
forgot God's commandments. If one god is good then three or four
gods must be even better, they thought. So they broke their covenant
with God and brought sacrifices to the clay and stone gods of their
neighbors as well as to the God of Israel. As punishment God stopped
helping the Israelites. The Philistines and other enemies were able to
beat them in battle.

The Philistines ruled the land when Samson was a judge. He was a
powerful man. Once he tore apart a lion with his bare hands. And he
killed a thousand Philistines using the jawbone of a donkey as a club.
Samson's strength came from his long hair. He never cut it because he
was a Nazirite, a servant of God. But Samson fell in love with Delilah. She
was a sly woman who finished his fighting career. Foolishly, he told
Delilah the secret of his strength. And one night, as Samson slept, Delilah
called in the Philistines to cut off his hair. Mighty Samson became weak
as a puppy. His enemies chained him, poked out his eyes, and made him
a slave.

Time passed and Samson's hair slowly grew back. He felt his strength
returning. One day the Philistines brought him to their temple in Gaza to
make fun of him. He reached out and felt the pillars that held up the

roof, "God, give me strength just this last time," he pleaded. With a great shove he toppled the pillars. The roof crashed down and Samson and his enemies died together.

The Holy Ark that the Israelites had carried in the desert now rested in the town of Shiloh in the center of the land. People came to Shiloh to pray and bring gifts to God. A childless woman called Hannah came and cried before the altar, begging God to help her and her husband to have a baby. "I promise that if I have a baby boy I will bring him here to Shiloh and let him serve You," she said. Hannah's prayer was answered. She had a baby and named him Samuel. When he was very young, Hannah brought Samuel to Shiloh to live with the priests. The little boy grew up to become a judge, a priest, and a prophet who spoke to God.

During Samuel's time, the tribes of Israel were strong and united. They drove the Philistines out of their land, made peace with other enemies, and followed God's laws.

Kings, for Better and for Worse

Samuel's sons became judges when Samuel grew old. But they were dishonest judges who cheated and took bribes. The people called out to Samuel angrily, "We don't want any more judges! All the other countries have kings. Get us a king too!"

"You'll be sorry," Samuel warned them. But he finally gave in and chose Saul, a tall, shy young shepherd, to be the first king of Israel. It was a sad, bad choice. Saul was a brave leader and a good fighter, but he once disobeyed Samuel. Then Samuel got angry and turned away from the young king. Without Samuel's help Saul became frightened, unhappy, and suspicious of everybody. Saul's helpers brought a red-headed boy named David to play the harp for Saul to cheer him up. The music helped Saul for a while.

David was brave as well as musical. He fought the Philistine giant, Goliath, and killed him. When David became a soldier and led the Israelites to a great victory, Saul grew jealous. "He wants to take my kingdom," said Saul. He tried to kill David. David escaped and Saul followed him, still trying to kill him. It was only after unhappy King Saul and his son Jonathan were killed in battle that David came back to the Kingdom of Israel.

Red-headed David became the second king of Israel. He was called "the sweet singer of Israel" because he wrote wonderful songs and poems, as you'll see in the next chapter. But he spent most of his time fighting wars. He crushed Israel's enemies and made the country larger and stronger than it had ever been. David captured Jerusalem and made it the capital of Israel. He brought the Ark of the Covenant to Jerusalem in a happy, singing and dancing parade of Israelites. But it was in Jerusalem that he broke God's laws and was punished.

David fell in love with Bathsheba, a woman who was married to Uriah, an officer in David's army. King David sent Uriah off to be killed in battle so that he could marry Bathsheba.

Even kings must obey God's laws. Because of David's evil deed, God sent the prophet Nathan to punish him. Nathan told the king this story:

"There were two neighbors in a city. One was a rich man with large flocks of sheep. The other was a poor man who had only one small lamb. The poor man raised the lamb in his home with his children and he loved it very much. One day a guest came to visit the rich man. The rich man went next door, grabbed the poor man's only lamb and slaughtered it to prepare a meal for his guest."

What Good Are Spiders?

When David was being hunted by King Saul, he hid in a cave. God sent a spider to spin a web across the cave opening. When Saul and his soldiers raced up to search the cave they saw the perfect web. "Nobody could be hiding in here," said King Saul, "the web isn't broken." The spider saved David's life.

—A LEGEND FROM THE TALMUD

David was very angry when he heard the story. He cried, "The rich man should be punished with death for his deed!" Then Nathan pointed at the king and thundered, "You are that man. And you will be punished!"

David and Bathsheba's first baby died. Maybe this was God's punishment. But another son, Solomon, became king after David died. Solomon was the wise, happy king of a strong country. During his time,

Seven Hundred Wives???!!!

Many men in the days of the Bible had more than one wife. But King Solomon broke Bible records with his 700 wives and 300 concubines. He often married princesses of other countries as a way of making agreements with the rulers of those lands. The custom of marrying several wives became less usual as the years went by. Finally, in 1000 C.E., Rabbi Gershom in Germany decreed—one wife per husband and one husband per wife.

Israelites lived in peace under their grapevines and fig trees. Solomon built a golden Temple for God in Jerusalem. He brought the Ark to the Temple and placed it in a special room called the Holy of Holies. Israelites came from all over the land to celebrate Sukkot, Passover, and Shavuot at the Temple. Solomon's ships traveled across the sea and brought back ivory, precious stones, spices, and even monkeys and peacocks. A queen came from faraway Sheba bringing gifts. Kings of distant countries made treaties with Israel. And Solomon made the treaties even stronger by marrying princesses from all those countries.

Sounds terrific . . . but all those wives and ships and fancy buildings caused some problems. Solomon built altars for the gods of all his wives. He built beautiful palaces and hired many servants and cooks and craftsmen. The people of Israel began to pay heavy taxes to support all of the king's projects. When Solomon died after a long reign, everyone hoped that his son, the new king, would cut their taxes. "Are you kidding?" laughed Solomon's son, Rehoboam, "I'm going to make you pay even more!"

"Forget it! We quit!" said the leaders of ten of the Hebrew tribes. They quickly formed their own kingdom which they called Israel. And greedy Rehoboam was left with just two and a half tribes in the tiny kingdom of Judah, with Jerusalem as its capital.

Map showing split into Judah and Israel

ASSYRIA

Dan

Lake Kinneret

ISRAEL

Jordan River

Shechem

Jerusalem

JUDAH

Dead Sea

Hebron

EGYPT

The Divided Kingdom

Prophets Spoke for God

While the kings of Israel were making wars or build-ing cities and the merchants were buying or selling and the children were playing or taking care of the sheep and goats . . . the prophets were talking to God. Then, following God's orders, they tried to teach the people to live by the laws of the Torah. In the marketplaces, the city gates, and the Temple courtyards, men and women like Nathan, Elijah, Huldah, Isaiah, and Jeremiah stood and shouted their warnings. "Be honest and generous with each other. Worship the One God and obey God's laws," they cried. The prophets were everyone's con-science.

Prophets with Problems

In the kingdoms of Israel and Judah some Jews again forgot God's laws. On mountain tops they built altars and brought sacrifices to idols made of wood or stone. Sometimes they even burned their children as gifts to the idols. Poor people became poorer. Rich people became richer. Merchants cheated. And the kings piled taxes on everyone.

God called to a few strong, good men and women and ordered them to teach Torah and become prophets to the kingdoms of Israel and Judah. "Warn the people that they're doomed if they disobey My laws," God told the prophets.

None of the prophets wanted the hard job that God offered them. But they did as they were told. Only the prophet Jonah refused to follow orders. God told him to go to Nineveh, a city in Assyria, and warn people to behave themselves. Instead, Jonah jumped aboard a boat and tried to escape God's orders. God sent a ferocious storm that nearly sank the boat. The other passengers dumped Jonah overboard where he was immediately swallowed by a huge fish, maybe a whale. From out of the fish's belly Jonah cried to God for help. "Okay, okay—I give up. I'll go to Nineveh!" The smart fish spat him out onto the shore, and Jonah trudged off to do his job.

Who shall go up to the
  mountain of the Lord?
Who will stand in God's holy
  place?
The one who has clean hands
  and a pure heart,
who hasn't been boastful
  and vain or sworn falsely.
  PSALMS 24:3–4

He succeeded. The people of Nineveh heard God's warning and stopped being evil and violent. But Jonah was angry that he had been sent to save the city. He went to sulk outside Nineveh's walls. God made a plant grow tall and shade Jonah. The next day God sent a worm to attack the plant so that it died. This made Jonah even sadder and angrier. God said to him, "You are upset about a plant that lived for only one day. So shouldn't I be concerned to save a great city with many people and animals?"

Another prophet, Elijah, got into big trouble when he followed God's orders. King Ahab of Israel had married Jezebel, a princess of Tyre. She brought her god Baal to Israel as well as four hundred and fifty priests to serve him. God sent Elijah to challenge the priests of Baal. "Let's set up two altars on Mount Carmel, one for Baal and one for God," Elijah suggested. "We'll pile firewood and a sacrifice on each one, then we'll see whose wood will begin to burn first." A great crowd of Israelites came to watch the contest. The priests of Baal sang, danced, jumped about, and prayed—but not a spark appeared on their altar. When Elijah called out to God the wood and the sacrifice on God's altar burst into flames.

"Liars! Fakers!" cried the Israelites. Elijah and the Israelites jumped on the priests of Baal and killed them all. Queen Jezebel was furious with Elijah. "I'll kill him just as he killed my priests!" she cried. The prophet ran away and hid under a bush in the desert. He was alone, hungry, and miserable. He wished he were dead. But God would not let him rest. In a still, small voice God ordered Elijah to go back and teach and warn the people of Israel.

Prophets like Isaiah, Amos, and Micah scolded rich people. They stood in the market places, at the gates of the city walls, and even in the courtyard of the Holy Temple shouting God's message. "God despises your feasts and your sacrifices. God doesn't want gifts. Take care of each other, help the poor, observe the Sabbath. If not, you'll be destroyed by your enemies."

Israel and Judah Lose Out

The kings of Israel and Judah weren't listening to the prophets. They were busy with more "important" matters. Their small kingdoms were squeezed between two huge neighbors. To the north were the Assyrians and later the Babylonians. To the south was the old enemy—Egypt.

Israel and Judah fought hard to keep these enemies from taking over their countries. Finally the fierce Assyrians conquered the kingdom of Israel and carried its people away to live in foreign lands.

Now only Judah was left. But the country was in danger because, like Israel, Judah disobeyed God's laws and ignored the warnings of the prophets. Luckily, one day the high priest of the Temple in Jerusalem found a lost book of the Bible hidden in the Temple. "This is God's word," proclaimed the prophetess Huldah. The people of Judah stood in the Temple courtyard and listened as King Josiah read the book of laws to them. "We've done wrong!" they cried. "We have disobeyed God's laws. We're sorry." Then there was a great spring cleaning in the land of Judah. Idols were swept out of the Temple. The hilltop altars of the god Baal were torn down and Baal's priests were driven out of the land. Josiah and his people celebrated a happy Passover feast in Jerusalem.

Only a few years later, during the rule of King Zedekiah, the kingdom of Judah was in danger again. Nebuchadnezzar, king of Babylonia, was preparing to gobble up the country. Jeremiah the prophet stood at the Temple gate and cried, "Obey God's laws. Make peace with the Babylonians." But the generals of Judah would not listen. They wanted to fight the Babylonians. "We have to shut Jeremiah up. He's bad for the country's morale," they said. They arrested the prophet and dumped him into a deep pit. By the time King Zedekiah pulled him out, the Babylonians were already breaking down the walls of Jerusalem.

There was a bloody battle. The Temple was destroyed and many of the Judeans were dragged off to exile in Babylonia. They had lost everything—their homes, their Temple, and even the help of God.

Misery and Hope

It was a miserable time—a time when the prophets could've yelled, "We told you so! We warned you!"

This statue of Elijah stands high on Mount Carmel. The prophet is said to have set ablaze an altar to God and destroyed the priests of Baal on this spot. PHOTO COURTESY OF MORDY BURSTEIN

Instead they tried to give people hope. The prophet Ezekiel spoke for God and said, "I will ruin your land and scatter you among other peoples. But I will be with you. And one day I will open your graves and you will live. And I will put my spirit in you and place you in your own land." Those weren't words that made people feel cuddled and protected. They knew there were painful years ahead of them. But the words promised that God would help the Jews through their worst time and would finally bring them back to the land of Israel.

Many years later the prophet Micah made rosier promises. He said, "They (all nations) shall beat their swords into plowshares and their spears into pruning hooks. Nation shall not lift up sword against nation, nor shall they learn war anymore." Micah and God were thinking ahead to the time when all wars would end. People would stop making guns and bombs to kill each other. They would build and farm and live together enjoying God's world.

So the Book of Prophets is sad and happy. Sad, because the Jewish people found a homeland . . . and lost it; believed in the laws of the Torah . . . and forgot them; heard the prophets . . . and ignored them. How is the Book of Prophets happy? Because of God's promise that the Jews will return to their land and finally there will be a good, peaceful life for all the people of the world.

The Mystery of the Ten Lost Tribes

King Sargon of Assyria boasted that he had conquered and carried off all the people of Israel, ten of the original twelve Hebrew tribes. Only the tribes of Judah were left, living close to the Temple in Jerusalem.

And truly, the ten tribes seemed to be swallowed up. No one ever saw them again. "But they can't be gone. It's impossible," the remaining Jews said to each other." God would never let so many of the Chosen People disappear. Someplace our lost Jewish brothers and sisters are living in a new Jewish land. We have to find it."

For centuries afterwards, as Jewish merchants and scholars traveled from country to country they kept an eye open, always looking for the ten lost tribes. In the ninth century Eldad the Danite was shipwrecked off Ethiopia. When he finally got home, he reported finding a land where the streets were filled with gold and silver and all the residents studied Torah and obeyed the Torah's laws. "Of course," people nodded, "those are the ten lost tribes."

Later a story was told about little red Jews who lived beyond a raging river called the Sambatyon. The river rested and could be crossed only on Shabbat. But no Jew would cross a river on Shabbat, the day of rest. So the little red Jews were left undisturbed.

The first Europeans to reach North America hoped that the American Indians might be the descendants of the ten lost tribes. To their disappointment the Indians wouldn't answer the greeting of "Shalom Aleikhem."

Where can we search now that the earth is all explored? Jews will have to look to the moon or Mars. Who can tell where those tribes may have gone?

Color a Bible Picture

Color King Solomon's Golden Temple

In Chapters Five and Six of the First Book of Kings, the Bible tells us how Solomon built the Temple. Copy this page on a copying machine and color it for your own picture of Solomon's great Temple.

4 About Lions, Beauty Contests, Poets, and More

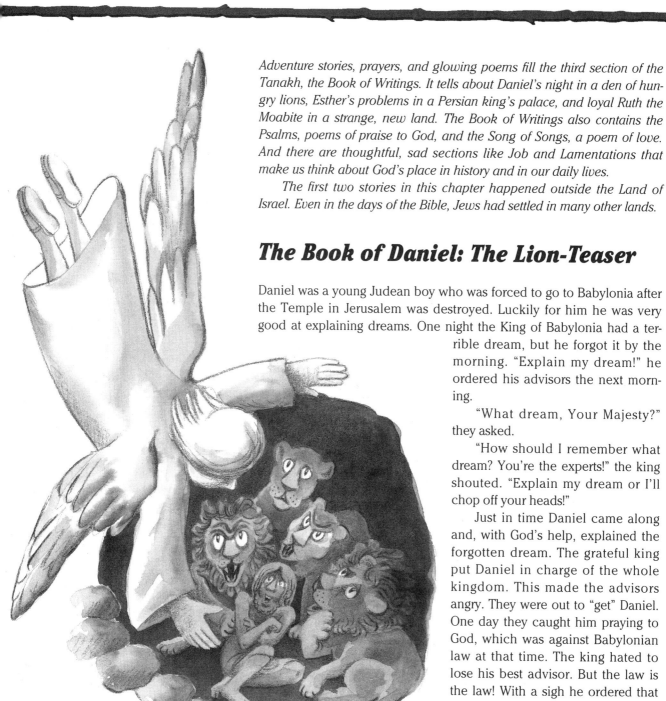

Adventure stories, prayers, and glowing poems fill the third section of the Tanakh, the Book of Writings. It tells about Daniel's night in a den of hungry lions, Esther's problems in a Persian king's palace, and loyal Ruth the Moabite in a strange, new land. The Book of Writings also contains the Psalms, poems of praise to God, and the Song of Songs, a poem of love. And there are thoughtful, sad sections like Job and Lamentations that make us think about God's place in history and in our daily lives.

The first two stories in this chapter happened outside the Land of Israel. Even in the days of the Bible, Jews had settled in many other lands.

The Book of Daniel: The Lion-Teaser

Daniel was a young Judean boy who was forced to go to Babylonia after the Temple in Jerusalem was destroyed. Luckily for him he was very good at explaining dreams. One night the King of Babylonia had a terrible dream, but he forgot it by the morning. "Explain my dream!" he ordered his advisors the next morning.

"What dream, Your Majesty?" they asked.

"How should I remember what dream? You're the experts!" the king shouted. "Explain my dream or I'll chop off your heads!"

Just in time Daniel came along and, with God's help, explained the forgotten dream. The grateful king put Daniel in charge of the whole kingdom. This made the advisors angry. They were out to "get" Daniel. One day they caught him praying to God, which was against Babylonian law at that time. The king hated to lose his best advisor. But the law is the law! With a sigh he ordered that

Daniel be thrown into a den of hungry lions. Roaring, yowling, and licking their lips the lions waited. Just in time God sent an angel to join Daniel in the den. "Shut your mouths!" said the angel to the lions. All night the lions glared hungrily at their "dinner." But they didn't dare touch Daniel. The Bible doesn't tell us if Daniel slept well. The lions' stomachs must have been growling pretty loudly. In the morning the king set Daniel free.

The Book of Esther: Esther Risks Her Life

Brave Queen Esther is the star of the feasting, masquerading holiday of Purim. She lived in Shushan, the capital city of Persia. One day the king of Shushan held a beauty contest to choose a wife. Esther won and became the new queen. Her cousin Mordecai liked to spend time at the palace gate, and once, while sitting there, he heard about a plot to kill King Ahasuerus. He told Esther and she told the king, which saved his life.

One day Mordecai got into serious trouble. Haman, the prime minister, came by and commanded Mordecai to bow down to him. Mordecai replied, "Uh-uh!" Haman was insulted. When he discovered that Mordecai was a Jew, he persuaded King Ahasuerus to order that all the Jews in the kingdom should be killed. Then he prepared tall gallows so that he himself could hang the insulting Mordecai. Immediately, Mordecai sent a message to Esther at the palace saying, "Help!" This was the time when Esther had to be brave. By Shushan's law if she went to the king without being invited she might be put to death.

Esther spent a whole day fasting and praying. Then she put on her best perfume and her prettiest dress, plucked up her courage and knocked on the king's door. She was lucky, and so were the Jews of Persia, because he greeted her warmly. "I want to invite you and Haman to dinner tomorrow," she said sweetly. Ahasuerus was pleased. He loved to eat. Haman was pleased too. It was an honor to be invited to dine with the queen. But to his horror, at dinner the next day, Esther told the king of Haman's ugly plot to kill her and all her people. Ahasuerus was furious. "Haman shall be hanged on the gallows he prepared for Mordecai!" he proclaimed.

Why Is the Torah like Water?

Just as the water flows down from high places and goes to low places the Torah leaves proud, uppity people and stays with humble people.

—A JEWISH FOLK SAYING

The Jews of Shushan and of all Persia were saved. There was feasting and partying all through the land.

The Book of Ruth: A Stranger in a Strange Land

In the springtime when bright wildflowers covered the hillsides and farmers were cutting the first crop of wheat, Ruth and Naomi crossed into Israel from the land of Moab. Naomi was an Israelite woman who had gone to live in Moab with her husband and two sons. The sons married Moabite women. A while later Naomi's sons and husband died. Naomi missed her homeland and decided to leave her Moabite daughters-in-law, Orpah and Ruth, and return to Israel. But Ruth would not stay behind. "Please don't ask me to leave you," she begged. "Wherever you go I will go. Your land will be my land. Your God will be my God." Naomi hugged Ruth and they came to Israel together.

They were very poor, so Naomi sent Ruth to the field to gather the grain the farmers had left. Boaz, the owner of the field, saw Ruth. "Who is that beautiful woman?" he asked. "That's Naomi's daughter-in-law," his workers told him. "She is not only beautiful, but she is also a good, loyal person. She wouldn't let Naomi return to Israel alone." Boaz helped Ruth gather grain. They fell in love, were married, had children, and lived happily together. And one of their great-grandchildren was David, the second king of Israel.

Why did God make only two people, Adam and Eve?

So that no one could say, "My parents are better than your parents."

The story of Ruth, Boaz, and Naomi is acted and retold again and again. Here are a modern Ruth and Boaz on a Galilee hillside. PHOTO COURTESY OF RIVKA DORFMAN

Every Shavuot when the first wheat is ripening in the Land of Israel and the hills are bright with flowers, we remember the story of Ruth, Naomi, and Boaz.

Psalms: In Praise of God

Red-haired King David, the second king of Israel, was a musician and a poet as well as a great soldier. Many believe that David wrote the section of the Book of Writings called Psalms. The psalms describe the power and greatness of God and tell of the writer's love of God. Over the centuries people have whispered the words of David's twenty-third psalm to give themselves courage when they were sad or frightened and needed help.

> The Lord is my shepherd
> I will not lack.
> God lets me lie down in green pastures,
> Leads me beside peaceful waters,
> Restores my soul.
> God guides me in the right paths, for God's name's sake.
>
> —PSALM 23

Another verse from Psalms became a happy Hebrew song that you may know: "Hinei Mah Tov."

> See how good and pleasant it is
> For brothers and sisters to live together.
>
> —PSALM 133

The Bible seems to jump from happy to sad thoughts, and then back again.

Psalm 137 is full of tears. It was sung by Jews who had been captured by their enemies, the Babylonians, and were being taken far away from their homes.

Corners for Poor People

Jewish farmers didn't cut the grain in the corners of their fields. Bible law required that the grain in the corners be left for the poor.

By the rivers of Babylon we sat and cried when we rememberd Zion.
We hung our harps on the willow trees, for those who carried us
      away asked us to sing. . . .
How shall we sing the Lord's song in a foreign land?
If I forget thee, oh Jerusalem, let my right hand forget its cunning.
If I don't remember thee let my tongue cleave to the roof of my
      mouth,
If I don't set Jerusalem above my greatest joy.

—PSALM 137

Getting Mad

When Mordecai got angry at Haman, or Michal, David's wife, wanted to yell at David they didn't have many nasty words to choose from. Biblical Hebrew has only phrases like "yimach shimchah" or "lech la-Azazel."

Lech la-Azazel means "go to Azazel!" At Yom Kippur the poor goat that carried the sins of the Jewish people was brought to a rock called Azazel, deep in the desert.

Yimach shimchah means "may your name be erased" (from the book of life)!

Modern Hebrew adopted juicy curses from Arabic, Ladino, and Yiddish.

Proverbs: Advice from Wise King Solomon

King Solomon, the third king of Israel, begged God for one gift—wisdom. He was a lucky man because he also became the richest, best-loved, and most powerful of Israel's kings. People have found good advice in Solomon's Book of Proverbs since Bible times. Which of these proverbs makes sense to you?

+ A person who understands is slow to get angry.
+ A gossip separates close friends.
+ To do justice is more acceptable to God than sacrifices.
+ Better is a meal of greens (a poor, simple meal) where there is love than a fattened ox (an expensive meat meal) where there is hatred.
+ A person who is too lazy to plow in cold weather will go hungry and beg for food at harvest time.
+ One who digs a pit (to trap someone else) shall fall into it.
+ When there is no vision (no beliefs or goals) people become rebellious. But those who keep the Torah are happy.

The Song of Songs

The Song of Songs may have been written by Solomon too. It's a poem of love . . . maybe love for a woman, maybe love for God. The experts disagree. But it brings us the sweet, green smells of budding flowers and grasses in early spring time.

> Rise up my love, my fair one and come away!
> For the winter is past, the rain is over and gone.
> The flowers appear on the earth . . . the fig tree
>   makes green figs,
> And the blossoming vines smell sweet.

Lamentations: The Prophet Jeremiah Cries

Remember the sad story of the prophet Jeremiah in the last chapter? He tried to convince King Zedekiah and his generals to make peace with the Babylonians, but they wouldn't listen. Zedekiah was defeated, and Jeremiah sat and cried while the Babylonians destroyed the Temple and the city of Jerusalem. All his tragic prophecies had come true. Since that time, Jews have recited these words of Jeremiah's Lamentations while they cried for the lonely, ruined city of Jerusalem:

> How the city sits alone that was once full of people,
> How she has become like a widow,
> She that was great among nations, a ruler of lands,
> How she has become a servant. . . .
> All her friends . . . have become her enemies.

The Italian Renaissance artist Michelangelo painted the prophet Jeremiah sitting and mourning for the destroyed city of Jerusalem and its exiled people. PHOTO COURTESY OF DOV GUBITCH

Ezra and Nehemiah: Rebuilding the Temple and the Walls of Jerusalem

The Book of Prophets ended as the Jews were driven into exile in Babylonia. The section of Writings called 'Ezra and Nehemiah' tells how a new king of Babylonia allowed the Jews to come back to Jerusalem. Many Jews happily loaded their camels and donkeys and made their way back. But they found their Temple gone. Lizards and jackals scurried over its black, broken stones. New people had settled on their lands and in their homes. When the Jews began to rebuild their Temple the newcomers fought with them and tried to stop them.

Ezra, a Jewish scribe and scholar came from Babylonia to help his people. Nehemiah, a high official in the palace of the king of Shushan in Persia, also came. He led the Jews in rebuilding the walls around Jerusalem. They had to work holding a hammer in one hand and a sword in the other to fight off their enemies.

It was almost time for the Sukkot holiday when the building was finished. The tired people gathered at the Temple gate and Ezra read the Torah aloud and explained its words. Then each family built a sukkah and feasted. At the shiny, new Temple the Levites sang, played harps, and blew on the great, silver trumpets to celebrate.

The Cylinder of King Cyrus
Babylonians wrote their laws and records on clay tablets and cylinders. This cylinder message, written 2,400 years ago, tells that King Cyrus allowed all the captive people in his empire to go home and rebuild their temples. (The cuneiform, wedge-shaped, writing is not copied exactly so please don't try to read it.) We know from the books of Ezra and Nehemiah in the Bible that many Jews happily went back to Judea.

The Book of Chronicles: A Summing-Up

"Chronicles," the last section of the Book of Writings, is like the review your teacher gives before a big test. It starts with Adam, the first person, and follows the whole Bible story. It names the hundreds of people who appear in the Bible—from Amaziah to Mushi to Zavad—with countless others in between. At the end, Chronicles tells how the people of Judea came back from Babylonia to their land and to Jerusalem.

Technical Stuff

Remember, in Chapter Two you read that the Bible is divided into three sections: 1. Five Books of Moses; 2. Prophets; and 3. Writings.

The names of the Five Books of Moses are Genesis, Exodus, Leviticus, Numbers, and Deuteronomy.

Prophets are divided into Judges, Samuel One and Two, and Kings One and Two. Also in Prophets are the books of fifteen prophets. Isaiah, Jeremiah, and Ezekiel head the list.

Writings are divided into thirteen books. Some of the best known are Psalms, Song of Songs, Ruth, and Esther.

Each of the Bible's books is divided into chapters. Each chapter is divided into verses. That makes it easy to pinpoint a line or section. For instance, if you want to read about Noah and the flood, look up the Book of Genesis, Chapter Seven, Verses One to Twenty-Four—or—Genesis 7:1–24.

At last a happy ending! Well . . . not exactly an ending. It's true that the Bible ends right here with Chronicles. But the story of Torah goes on. The laws and wisdom of the Jewish people which grew out of the Bible keep growing. There's lots more to this story. You'll find some of it in Chapter Eight.

The Beauty of Simple Things
A Legend of the Talmud

One of the musical instruments used in the Temple was a reed pipe. It was smooth and slim and dated back to the days of Moses.

Since it was so valuable, the king ordered that the pipe be covered with gold. But afterward, the pipe lost its clear, sweet tone. So the craftsmen took off the gold and the pipe's voice sounded as sweet as before.

Copper cymbals were also used in the Temple service. When they were struck together they made a wonderful sound. One day the cymbals were damaged. Metal workers mended them and laid gold on them. But then, when one cymbal was struck against the other, the sound was harsh. So they took off the gold and the voice of the cymbals became as melodious as it had been.

Events of Bible Times

What was happening in the Land of Israel, among the neighbors around the Mediterranean Sea, and in the world? Here's a quick view:

"c." means a date that is approximate, not exact.

Year	In the Land of Israel
From 4000 to 3000 B.C.E.	
From 3000 to 2000 B.C.E.	Canaanite tribes live in the land

Year	In the Land of Israel
From 2000 to 1000 B.C.E.	God makes a covenant with Abraham Era of Hebrew patriarchs and matriarchs c. 1700—Hebrew tribes settle in Egypt c.1300—Moses leads the exodus of Hebrews to the Promised Land Era of Judges—Joshua, Deborah, Samson, Samuel, etc. c. 1020—Saul becomes first king
From 1000 to 800 B.C.E.	c. 1000–922—United Kingdom under King David and King Solomon c. 950—Solomon builds First Temple Kingdom divides into Judea and Israel Prophets Elijah, Isaiah, Micah, Amos, and others prophesy
From 800 to 600 B.C.E.	c. 722—Israel Conquered by Assyria, people sent into exile Prophets Huldah and Jeremiah prophesy
From 600 to 400 B.C.E.	586—Fall of Judea and exile of Judeans to Babylonia First Temple destroyed Prophets Ezekiel and Second Isaiah prophesy 538—Persians let Jews return and rebuild Temple Ezra and Nehemiah help rebuild the Temple and Jewish religious life

Around the Mediterranean Sea	In the World
	Creation—as described in the Book of Genesis, in the Bible
Kingdoms of Egypt and Sameria are founded	Chinese develop the wheel, plough, calendar, etc.
Copper and bronze begin to be used	Dravidians in India build large cities
c. 2500—Egyptian pyramids are built	
The alphabet is developed by the Canaanite/ Phonicians	
c. 1900–1600—ancient Babylonian Kingdom rises and falls	Aryans conquer India and establish caste system
c.1600—Use of iron begins	Shang dynasty rules China for 600 years
c. 1300—Assyrian Empire rises	
c. 1200—Trojan War between Greece and Rome	

Aramaeans and Hittites build cities in Syria	Chow dynasty rules China for nearly 1,000 years

c. 776—Olympic games begin in Greece	Buddhist religion develops in India
c. 750—City of Rome is founded	
Assyria conquered by Babylonia	551—Confucius is born in China
Babylonia conquered by Persians	c. 500—Japanese Empire is founded
Golden Age of art, drama, and philosophy in Greece	
c. 509—Roman Empire is founded	

Bible Crafts: Make a Costume

Are you doing a Bible play?
Do you need a costume for a Purim party?
Here is how to dress up as Abraham, Sarah, and other patriarchs and matri-
archs.

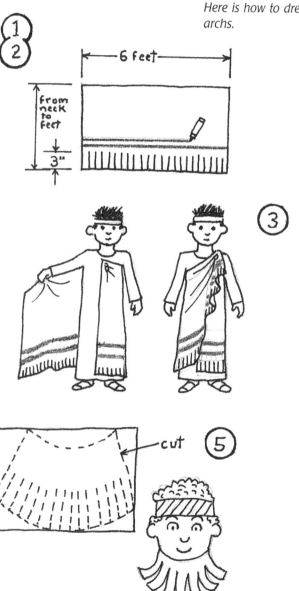

For Abraham you will need:

> an old, light-colored sheet, tablecloth, or curtain
> colored marking pens
> a long-sleeved night shirt or nightgown
> 2 safety pins
> sandals
> tennis headband
> a staff—thick branch or broomstick as long as a
> cane
> for a beard—cotton batting or construction paper
> scissors
> measuring tape
> adhesive tape

1. Cut the sheet so that it's 6 feet long and as wide as the measurement from your neck to your feet.
2. Cut the fringes 3 inches deep along one of the long edges. Above the fringes draw two stripes with a blue marking pen.
3. Put on the night shirt. Hold the sheet with the fringed edge down, parallel to the ground, and pin one of the top corners to the middle of your night shirt. Wrap the rest of the sheet under your left arm, around your back, under your right arm, and across your chest. Pin it to the left shoulder of your night shirt and let the end hang down.
4. To make Abraham's beard of cotton pull the cotton into a beard shape and tape it to your chin and under your ears.
5. To make the beard of paper, cut a 9 x 12 inch sheet of paper as shown. Cut fringes on the bottom edge. Curl the fringes gently using the side of a pencil. Tape it to your chin and under your ears.
6. If you want a mustache, you can tape it on or attach it to your nose like Rebecca's nose ring (see

explanation below). To make a nose ring or nose
mustache use stiff paper and cut as shown.

For Sarah you will need:

> For a tunic—an old, light-colored sheet, tablecloth,
> or curtain
> colored marking pens
> a long-sleeved night shirt or nightgown
> sandals
> bracelet, ankle bracelet, and stiff paper for nose
> ring (see illustration)
> head scarf—about 12 inches wide and 3 or 4 feet
> long
> wide strip of cloth or bright scarf for sash
> scissors
> ruler

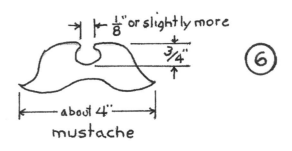

mustache

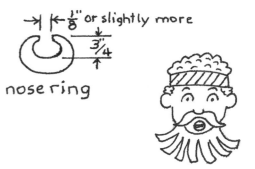

nose ring

1. To make Sarah's tunic cut the sheet so that it is as
   wide as your shoulders, about 20 inches.
2. Fold it in half. Cut an opening large enough for
   your head in the center of the fold (see illustra-
   tion).
3. Use the markers to make bright stripes and
   designs on the tunic. Cut fringes at the bottom
   edge.
4. Put on the night shirt.
   Put on the tunic over
   the night shirt and tie
   it at the waist with
   the sash.
5. Make the nose ring
   as shown (the Bible
   tells us that Sarah's
   daughter-in-law,
   Rebecca, wore a
   nose ring). Put on the
   jewelry and the head
   scarf. You can pin the
   scarf together at the
   back of your neck to
   hold it in place.

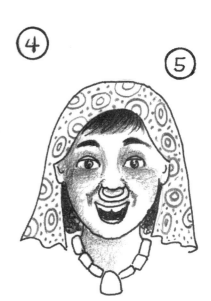

5

Kids in the Bible

Bearded men wearing sandals and white robes wander through the pages of the Bible. They're busy talking to God, or arguing about God with other people, or being scolded by God. You have to look very carefully to find stories about boys and girls. They're in there. But sometimes a long story is told in only a few words. Your imagination has to fill in the gaps.

Here are stories about three Bible kids—Miriam, Samuel, and David—with the gaps filled in.

Miriam's Longest Night

As the Bible tells it:

> When the Hebrews were slaves in Egypt the pharaoh (king) of Egypt grew afraid that they were becoming too strong. He ordered that all the Hebrew boy babies should be drowned in the Nile River. Pharaoh commanded, "Every son that is born you shall throw into the river." And a woman had a son . . . and hid him for three months. When she could no longer hide him she took a basket . . . and put the child in it, and she laid it in the rushes by the river's edge. And his sister stood nearby to know what would be done to him.
>
> —EXODUS 1:22, 2:2–5

Our story adds:

Thistles slashed at her legs as Miriam stumbled along the moonlit path. The big, straw basket she carried kept catching on the bushes. Twice she nearly fell. But she grabbed the basket more tightly and hurried on. Her mother walked ahead of her carrying the baby. Suddenly Miriam heard the sound of rushing water ahead. It was the river. The terrible Nile River that had gulped down so many baby boys! With a squeak she bumped into her mother at the river's edge. "Ssshhhh," hissed her mother. "Put the basket here in the clearing."

Miriam set the basket against a clump of reeds. She could feel squishy mud between her toes. Her mother kneeled, laid the baby in the basket, and tucked a cloth around him. He pulled out a plump arm, stretched, and curled up to sleep again.

"I'll take care of him, Mama," Miriam whispered. "Don't worry." Miriam's mother hugged her tightly. The little girl felt the wetness of her mother's tears on her own cheek.

"I know you'll take care of him," said her mother. "And remember, when the princess comes to bathe in the morning make sure she finds the baby. She'll love him. I know she'll love him. She won't let him be drowned."

She turned quickly and Miriam heard her climbing up the bank. Then Miriam heard only rustling reeds and the rushing, hungry river. "There's n-nothing t-to be scared a-b-b-out," she whispered aloud, trying to convince herself. Just to be sure, her fingers searched the damp sand and found a broken willow branch and a handful of stones. Holding her "weapons" tightly, she sat on a pile of reeds and waited.

Frogs began to croak at each other. Crickets creaked. Then a mosquito started to whine around and around her nose. All right, mosquito, she thought. Just help me stay awake. She counted backward, slapped at the mosquito, pinched her arms . . . and still her eyelids began to droop. "Stay up . . . just . . . a . . . little longer . . . " she murmured, and fell asleep.

Suddenly Miriam's eyes snapped open! The sky was blue-gray. The crickets and frogs were silent. Everything was silent—too silent. She blinked and squinted and then she saw it. A brownish-gray, catlike shape was crouched against the reeds. No, Miriam realized with horror, it was too big to be a cat. It was a desert lion. The tip of the animal's tail thrashed back and forth. Then it began to move noiselessly, flat on its belly toward the basket.

"Yeeeowwww!" screeched Miriam, jumping up. Fierce, yellow eyes turned toward her. The lion snarled and its fangs shone in the dawn light. One, two, three—Miriam flung the stones right into the snarling face. She snatched up the willow branch and swung it, screaming, "Get away! Get out!" The big cat reared up on its hind legs, spitting and baring its teeth. It was as tall as Miriam. But she kept swatting with the branch and screaming. The noise woke the baby who started howling and kicking, rocking the basket from side to side.

All the commotion was too much for the lion. He had probably only planned on a small dessert with no fuss. He dropped to the ground, shaking his head in disgust, backed up, and slunk away along the bank with his tail dragging. Miriam picked up her little brother. She hugged him with one arm and rocked back and forth. In her other hand she held the branch tightly. She glared around the circle of reeds ready to fight whatever might come next.

The sky brightened. Birds woke and flitted through the reeds. The rising sun slanted across the river and warmed Miriam's tightly clenched body. Then at last she heard girls' voices calling out and laughing. White linen dresses sparkled on the path leading to the river. One young woman walked in front under a fringed, straw umbrella.

"The princess!" Miriam gasped. She quickly put the baby into the basket and pushed it out onto the bare sand at the edge of the water. Then she ducked back into the reeds. With a "Wa-a-aaa-aaaa!" the baby woke up. Where was breakfast? He was awake and ready to eat. "Waaaaah!" he wailed indignantly.

Miriam heard the chatter of surprised voices, then the sound of splashing as one of the girls waded along the river and found the basket. She carried it back to the group. "Please baby, smile at them," Miriam whispered. Like magic the wailing stopped. There was a chorus of oohs and aahs. And a clear commanding voice rose above the others, saying, "He's beautiful. Look, he's smiling at me! He must be a Hebrew boy baby. And he's hungry. Poor little thing. We'd better take care of him."

Bursting with joy Miriam jumped out onto the sand. "Good morning Your Majesty, princess," she cried. "Shall I go and get you a nurse from among the Hebrew women to feed the baby?"

Miriam's long, scary night of watching was over. We all know the rest of the story. Baby Moses grew up and led the Jews to the Promised Land. But who knows, if not for Miriam it might never have happened.

Samuel All Alone

As the Bible tells it:

> In the days of the judges, a woman called Hannah came to worship
> at Shiloh. She cried bitterly because she had no children. In her
> prayers she begged God to help her so that she would have a baby.
>
> "Oh Lord . . . if You will remember me . . . and You will give your
> handmaiden a manchild I will send him to serve God all the days of
> his life. . . . Hannah bore a son and named him Samuel. . . . The
> woman nursed her son, and when she had weaned him she took
> him up with her . . . and brought him to the house of the Lord at
> Shiloh. . . . And the child served the Lord before Eli the priest.
>
> —FIRST BOOK OF SAMUEL 1:11, 1:20, 1:24, 2:12

Our story adds:

Sometimes Samuel got so angry he wanted to smash one of the oil
lamps! He didn't want to be here in the house of God. He wanted to be at
home like other kids his age. "Is it my fault that my mom couldn't have a
baby?" he'd think. How could she give me away as if I were a goat or a
basket of onions? And then he'd stamp through the dark rooms of the
Temple and kick at pebbles while he did his chores.

Eli the priest always knew when Samuel was angry. Eli was almost
blind. He couldn't see Samuel's red face or his scowl, but he knew. Then
he'd call Samuel to sit and read aloud to him from the ancient scrolls.
"It's a great honor to serve in God's house, my son," he would say gently.
"Be grateful that you've been chosen."

In the middle of reading, one of Eli's sons would call, "Samuel, fill the
oil lamps," or "Boy, sweep the bloody sand up from around the altar and
get some clean sand," or, "Sam, polish the menorahs." And Samuel
would be off and running again.

Yeuch!—the two people he didn't like the most were Eli's two sons.
Not because they made him work, but because they were thieves. They
were Temple priests so you'd expect them to be honest. But Samuel
watched as the sons cheated people who brought sacrifices to God. They
would take more than the priest's share of the meat or grain. Then the
people would be left with nothing for themselves. How could God let
them get away with that?

One day Samuel watched as a worshiper protested that the priests

After Joshua and the
Hebrews conquered Canaan
the town of Shiloh became
the religious center for the
people of Israel. The Ark of
the Covenant rested there.
Much later the town of
Shiloh was destroyed by an
enemy army. Archaeologists
believe they have found the
ruins of ancient Shiloh in the
hills near Jerusalem.

were taking too much meat. The Temple guards beat him and threw him out of the Temple gate. Samuel couldn't fall asleep that night. He curled up under the coat his mother had made for him. It smelled of the fields of grain and the vineyards and wild flowers of his home village. The coat always made him feel better. But tonight it just made him lonely. I don't belong here, he thought. Even God doesn't belong here because Eli's sons keep breaking the laws.

Maybe God isn't in Shiloh anymore, he thought suddenly. Maybe God got disgusted and went away! Then he had another great idea. If God went away I can go home! He pictured his mother and father standing in the doorway of their small, stone house with the grapevines and olive trees all around. He could almost smell the pita bread baking. Suddenly the picture vanished as a deep voice broke into his dream.

"Samuel!" The voice filled the room.

Samuel jumped up and hurried through the stone passage to Eli's room. "Did you call me?" Samuel asked the priest.

"No my son," said Eli. "Go back to sleep."

Samuel raced back, fell onto his straw mat, and pulled up the coat. He wanted to get back to the warm dream of home. But again he heard, "Samuel!" Again he ran across the cold, stone floor to Eli's room. And again Eli sent him back to bed. Samuel squeezed his eyes shut and pulled the coat over his ears. But even with his ears covered he heard the deep voice call for the third time, "Samuel!"

This time when Samuel came to Eli, the old priest understood. "Go and lie down," he said. "When God calls you again you must say, 'Speak, God. Your servant is listening.'"

God!!! Calling me? Samuel's legs shook as he stumbled back to bed and lay shivering and waiting.

"Samuel! Samuel!"

"S-speak God, your servant is listening," Samuel whispered.

And God said to Samuel, "I will judge and punish the house of Eli. Eli's sons have sinned against Me. Gifts and sacrifices will never wash away the sins of the House of Eli!"

The voice ended. The room was still. But the wall beside Samuel trembled as though a great wind had passed through. He hugged his knees and tried to stop shaking. God spoke to me, he thought. Why? "God," he whispered, "why did You tell me about Eli? What do You want me to do?" There was no answer. But Samuel felt an answer tingling inside him. He whispered it aloud, "I will learn and grow and one day I will lead the people of Israel in place of Eli and his sons."

Now he knew why he was in Shiloh. It didn't make him happy. He was still lonely. But he knew that God was with him. Samuel took a deep breath, tucked his chin under the soft coat, and fell asleep.

Lonely, little Samuel grew up to be a powerful judge over the people of Israel and the first prophet. God spoke to Samuel many times. And God had Samuel choose Saul to be the first king of Israel, and David the second king.

The Pain in the Neck

As the Bible tells it:

> Saul was the first king of Israel. He led his army against many ene-
> mies. The worst enemies of all were the Philistines. The Philistines
> stood on a mountain on one side and Israel stood on a mountain on
> the other side. . . . A champion went out of the camp of the
> Philistines called Goliath . . . and he said, "I challenge the soldiers of
> Israel . . . give me a man to fight." Saul and all of Israel were very
> frightened. . . . And David said to Saul, "[I] your servant will go and
> fight this Philistine."
>
> —FIRST BOOK OF SAMUEL 17:3–11, 17:32

This big-nosed sling-shooter was carved into the stone wall of a Syrian palace about 850 B.C.E. David probably held his sling the same way when he aimed at Goliath.

Our story adds:

David's seven older brothers thought he was a pain in the neck. He had red hair and bright eyes. The girls all thought he was very cute. He sat around playing the lyre a lot, which the older people loved. (The lyre is a musical instrument—a frame with strings like a small harp.) His brothers thought it made boring music. It put them to sleep.

When David was sent out to watch the sheep and goats, he came home and told a wild story about killing a bear and a lion with his bare hands. "Fat chance," scoffed the brothers. But they really got annoyed when a messenger came from the royal court and called David to play the lyre for King Saul.

After that David knew he was special. A court musician, a fighter of lions and bears, and cute too.

David's three older brothers joined King Saul's army and went off to fight the Philistines—Israel's toughest enemy. They and the rest of the Israelites camped on a hillside above the Elah Valley. On the hill opposite them the army of the Philistines was encamped. Each morning a gigantic, powerful Philistine called Goliath swaggered out of his camp and roared across to the Israelites, "I challenge you to send someone out to fight me, man to man. If he kills me the Philistines will be your servants. If I kill him the Israelites will be our servants." And then he laughed a booming laugh that made the hair of every Israelite stand up with fear.

Nobody dared to fight the giant Goliath. That is, nobody dared until David arrived in the Israelite camp. He was bringing corn, bread, and cheese that his father had sent for his brothers.

"What's going on?" he asked when he heard Goliath's challenge.

"Oh keep quiet and mind your own business," said his brothers. "Go home."

But David was too stubborn and sure of himself to go home. "I can beat Goliath!" he said. Everyone argued with him. Even Saul tried to discourage him. "You're just a boy," said the king. "Goliath is an experienced fighter."

"God who saved me from the lion and the bear will save me again," said David.

"Not that story again," said his brothers, rolling their eyes.

David tried the king's armor and took the king's sword. He looked terrific, but he couldn't move. The armor was too heavy. So he stepped out of the armor and tucked his sling-shot and five smooth stones into his belt. Then he scrambled down the hill to face Goliath.

"Who is this red-headed kid?" roared Goliath as David reached the valley. "An Israelite brat? I'll tear him apart. I'll feed him to the jackals!"

David answered, "You come with a sword and a spear, but I come with God. God doesn't need weapons to win a battle." He set a stone in his sling and sent it flying right to the center of Goliath's forehead. With a great crash of armor the giant fell to the ground, out cold! David quickly pulled out Goliath's huge sword and hacked off his head. It was all over in seconds.

The Philistine army stood frozen for a moment. Then they dropped their weapons, turned, and ran. With cheers and shouts the army of Israelites charged across the valley, chased the Philistines over the mountain and out of the Land of Israel.

King Saul was so grateful that he gave his daughter Michal to David to marry. And he invited David to come and live at the royal court. That made David's parents very happy. And David's brothers were even happier. The kid was finally out of their hair.

Because David was so sure of himself, and because God was with him, he went on to become the second king of Israel. The Bible tells us that he was a great fighter, musician, poet, and lover. But that's another story. Go back to Chapter Three to read more about grown-up David.

Filling in the Gaps

Here and there in the Bible you'll find kids besides Miriam, Samuel, and David. There's quiet, patient Isaac (Genesis 22:1–13) and Jephthah's brave daughter (Judges 11:30–40), and Dinah, an only sister who grew up in a family of twelve brothers (Genesis 34), and the five gutsy daughters of Zelophehad (Numbers 27:1–8). Because the Bible tells a long story in very few words we don't know much about them. But you can do what Jews have been doing for centuries—you can add more. Choose a child in the Bible and put yourself in his or her place. Then write or draw a longer story for him or her.

Lessons and Legends

For centuries rabbis and teachers have added to Bible stories. Sometimes they used these longer stories to teach moral lessons called midrashim. Or sometimes they became exciting tales called aggadot, for storytellers. Midrashim and aggadot are still being written and collected wherever Jews live. Some stories that you thought came from the Bible are really aggadot, or legends, that were told long after the Bible was completed.

Here are two aggadot (adapted from the *Legends of the Bible* by Louis Ginzberg). The first is about Moses as a baby. The second tells of King Solomon, his daughter, and the stars.

Baby Moses

When Moses was a curious three-year-old living in Pharaoh's palace he pulled the crown off of Pharaoh's head and put it on his own head. Pharaoh's advisers were horrified. "That baby knew exactly what he was doing," they told Pharaoh. "If you don't get rid of him he'll steal your throne when he grows up!"

The angel Gabriel quickly disguised himself as one of Pharaoh's advisers. "Noble Pharaoh, you can test the child," he said. "Put a precious stone and a burning coal on the table in front of him. If he reaches for the precious stone you'll know that he understands what he's doing. Then you'll have to kill him. But if he reaches for the burning coal you'll know that he is just a baby who likes bright things and you'll let him live."

The king agreed and set up the test. Everyone watched breathlessly as Moses reached with his chubby hand. It moved toward the precious stone! The angel Gabriel invisibly shoved the baby's hand toward the burning coal. The baby grabbed the coal. Quickly, with a howl, he dropped it, stuck his hot hand into his mouth, and burned his tongue. That's why Moses stuttered for the rest of his life.

"Just a silly baby," said the Pharaoh with a smile. "He's no danger to me."

King Solomon's Daughter

King Solomon was so wise that he could read the stars to predict the future. One night he learned from the stars that his favorite daughter would marry a very poor man. "Never!" he proclaimed. He imprisoned his daughter in a high tower on an island in the middle of the sea. And he set seventy guards around the tower.

Soon after, on a bitterly cold night, a homeless, young man found the carcass of an ox in a field. He crept inside it to keep warm. A huge bird swooped down, lifted the carcass with the man inside and carried them to the roof of the princess's tower. There the bird perched and ate up the ox, leaving the man stranded.

When the princess came up to the roof in the morning for some exercise she found him. He was a bit smelly from his night inside the ox, but very handsome. The princess had him bathe and change his clothing. Then they chatted, got to know each other, and fell in love. The smart young man wrote a marriage agreement, and the couple called on God and the angels to be witnesses to their wedding.

Soon afterwards the princess became pregnant. The baffled guards who knew nothing of her husband sent for King Solomon. When the king arrived the princess happily introduced him to her new husband. "What a mistake I made to think I could fool the stars." said King Solomon. "But I won't complain. The boy is poor, but he's handsome, and wise too."

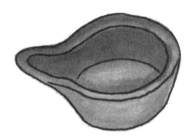

Bible Crafts: Make an Oil Lamp

Small oil lamps made of clay lit houses in the days of the Bible. Lamps like this one are found in the ruins of ancient towns all over Israel. A large oil lamp with six branches—a menorah—was used in the Temple.

If you plan to burn oil in your lamp buy a package of natural clay at an art supply store and follow directions 1–5.

If your lamp is for decoration only buy a quick-baking clay in a toy or crafts store and shape it as in directions 1–3; then bake it as directed on the package and decorate.

You will need:

> one pound of natural clay or quick-baking clay
> a board to work on
> acrylic paint and brush
> package of candle wicks (available at crafts store)
> 1/2 cup of olive oil or other cooking oil, to fill the lamp
> matches

Follow these steps:

1. Roll the clay and pound it on a board to knock out all the air bubbles.
2. Shape the clay into a ball about as big as an orange. Shape the ball into a lamp by pushing both thumbs into the middle and pulling the sides up. Keep the walls the same thickness or they will crack while drying.
3. Pinch the wall to make a tip that sticks out.

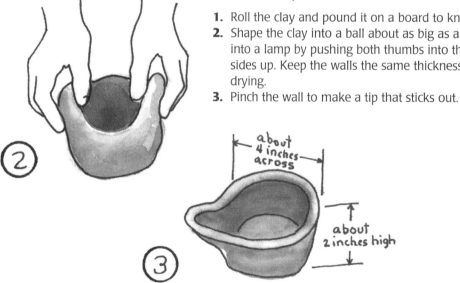

4. Wet your fingers and smooth the surface.
5. Let the lamp dry for a week—not in direct sunlight. Then have it fired (baked) in a kiln (pottery oven) in a ceramic store.
6. After firing you can paint the outside with acrylic paint.
7. When the paint is dry fill your lamp with oil. Put in the wick. Leave one end sticking out. Let the wick soak up oil for about 1/2 hour. Then light the outside end of the wick.

Make a Hanukkah Menorah

The holiday of Hanukkah isn't described in this book because it happened after the Bible was written. You can make a candle-lit Hanukkah menorah anyway. Make eight small oil lamps and one taller lamp. Glue the taller lamp in the center of a decorated base made of plywood or clay. It will be the *shammash*. Glue the small lamps to the board on each side of the tall lamp. Place a candle in each lamp.

What's Next?

How did Bible kids live? What games did they play . . . if they played? Move on to Chapter Six and get your feet and hands into the daily life of a Bible kid.

6 A Day in the Life of a Bible Kid

A Sleep-Over

You're in luck! You've been invited to a sleep-over at the home of two kids who lived in Bible times—Abigail and Ehud. They live in a village in the hills near Jerusalem. Don't pack dress-up clothing because you'll be helping out with the chores. And don't plan on playing computer games or watching videos.

Here are some of the things you'll do:

Guide a wooden plow that's pulled by oxen or bullocks.

Grind kernels of grain between two stones to make flour.

Push a stone roller across a house roof to compact and waterproof the roof.

Pick figs, grapes, olives, dates . . . whatever is ripe.

Take the sheep or goats to pasture.

Wait for me!

Separate wheat husks from the grain by tossing the wheat into the air.

Help the potter shape large storage jars out of clay.

Bring fruits and vegetables home from the field.

Carry jars of water from the well.

Squeeze grapes with your bare feet.

In an ancient mill in northern Israel this boy is leading a donkey around and around. The donkey is turning a huge stone which is squeezing oil out of olives in the space beneath it. A similar oil-pressing stone was dug up at the 2,000 year old village of Kfar Nahum on the shore of Lake Kinneret.

Wait—you're not done yet. You will also fill the oil lamps with olive oil; milk the goats and sheep; squeeze cheese into hard balls; help to make flatbread in a clay oven; trade your cheese, fruits, and vegetables for other goods in the marketplace; and more.

The tools made of wood and reeds that Abigail and Ehud used have crumbled and disappeared. They may have looked like more recent tools shown here. But many tools made of stone, bronze, and baked clay

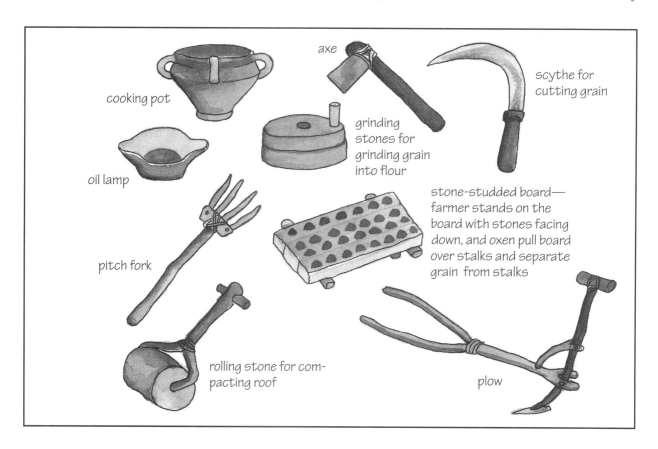

cooking pot

oil lamp

axe

grinding stones for grinding grain into flour

scythe for cutting grain

pitch fork

stone-studded board—farmer stands on the board with stones facing down, and oxen pull board over stalks and separate grain from stalks

rolling stone for compacting roof

plow

The Gezer Calendar

Little kids played with small, clay animals. Older kids learned to read from stone tablets like a farmer's calendar which was found at Gezer in Israel. Three thousand years ago a Hebrew boy or girl sang these words of the Gezer calendar as he or she herded the goats or planted seeds.

> His two months are olive harvest
> His two months are planting grain
> His two months are late planting
> His one month is hoeing the flax (linen cloth for clothing is
>   made from flax)
> His one month is harvesting the barley
> His one month is harvest and holiday
> His two months are vine-tending
> His month is summer fruit

have survived through the centuries. They are found by archaeologists in digs throughout Israel.

Take a Rest

Tch, tch, tch . . . you had a hard day of work. You may have blisters on your hands from grinding the flour. Your legs may be purple from the toes to the knees after pressing the grapes. And you're starving! You can hardly wait for supper even though you know it'll be balls of fermented goat cheese, salty olives, and chunks of chewy bread.

"Do you just work all the time?" you ask Ehud. "Not all the time," he laughs. He pulls a stone tablet from one of the wall niches. It has Hebrew letters carved into it. They don't look exactly like the letters you know. Hebrew writing has changed since Bible times. "I'm learning to read and write," Ehud tells you. Abigail shakes a sack of smooth, shiny stones and shows you how to play a game like checkers. The younger brothers and sisters push little animals and wagons made of clay around the floor. They look like the toys you used when you were small, but they're muddy brown, not bright plastic.

After supper comes the entertainment. No books, movies, TV, or CD-ROMs. The entertainment is Grandpa Uriah, the oldest member of the family. Everyone settles down in the courtyard around the hot coals of the cooking fire. The air is chilly so Grandpa Uriah wraps a sheepskin around his shoulders and starts to tell a story. "Many, many years ago there was no world. No sun or moon or stars. No goats or milk or cheese. No olive trees. There was only the spirit of God floating in the emptiness."

The family huddles close and listens to the story of how God made their green, beautiful world grow out of the emptiness. It's the first story of the Bible. At last Grandpa Uriah finishes with, "And God said, 'I did a good six days of work. Tomorrow, Shabbat, I'm going to rest!' "Grandpa Uriah stops to rest too. But Ehud begs, "Please tell about the great flood." Grandpa Uriah smiles and begins to tell about Noah, the crowded ark, the rain, the pigeon . . . but before he gets to the punchline you're almost asleep. So Abigail leads you inside to sleep on a straw mat.

Inside? Inside what? Let's look at the kinds of houses people lived in during the days of the Bible.

These toys made of clay were found in Jordan, Syria, and Israel. The two animals have hollow spouts and may have been baby bottles.

*Caves have been home to Israelis
since the cavemen. Bones and tools
of 200,000 year old Neanderthal
people were found here in the Amud
cave in Northern Israel.* PHOTO COURTESY
OF DOV GUBITCH

Home Sweet Home

A Cave

Caves were homes for poor people and hideouts for people who were running away from enemies. Elijah the prophet lived in a cave on Mount Carmel, near the modern city of Haifa. David and his friends hid in caves when they were escaping from King Saul. After Bible times, about 2,000 years ago, Jewish rebels against the Roman rulers of Judea lived in caves in the Judean desert.

Caves can be damp and drippy. In the wintertime the whole family may have cuddled together for warmth like a family of puppies. But the caves were warmer in the winter and cooler in the summer than the outside air. Sometimes the family shared their cave with a tribe of bats. When they made a little cooking fire on the dirt floor and put down a sheepskin rug, it felt like home.

A Tent

Abraham and Sarah, the first Jews, lived in tents made of cloth woven from the hair of goats and camels. Strong poles held the cloth up high in the middle. At the side it was fastened to pegs, or short sticks, which were hammered into the ground. There were big, fancy tents with bright rugs and cushions for rich people. And there were small tents for poor people. But in one important way all tents were alike. They were dry, shady homes which could be rolled up and carried.

Several times a year Abraham and Sarah would roll up their tents, load them onto donkeys or camels, and move to a new place. Like the Bedouin, the modern wandering shepherds, they led their flocks from waterhole to waterhole and from chewed-over pastures to juicy, new pastures.

*Bedouin Arabs like these in Southern
Israel live in tents. Many of them lead
their herds to a new pasture every
few months. Others have stopped
wandering and have taken jobs in
town. But they still like their tent
homes better than houses. The woman
on the right is grinding grain between
two stones—just like in the days of
the Bible.* PHOTO COURTESY OF ED TOBEN

A House of Stone or Mud Bricks

During the forty-year walk through the desert from Egypt to the Land of Israel the tribes of Israel probably lived in tents and shelters like a sukkah. When they crossed into the Promised Land they took over the houses of the Canaanites or settled beside them. They became farmers and townspeople and lived in solid houses made of mud brick or stone. If mud brick sounds like crumbly mud pies to you—would you believe that a 5,000-year-old gate made of mud is still standing? Mud bricks were a mixture of mud, straw, and lime. They were shaped into bricks and dried in the sun before they were used. Rooms were small and usually had no windows. The mud brick walls were plastered with a lime-mud mixture. The roofs of the houses were often tree branches laid close together and plastered over with a mixture of earth and lime. After the heavy winter rains the owner had to lift a stone roller to the roof to press the earth down and make it watertight again. Kitchens were breezy and wide open. The women cooked and baked in the courtyard in front of the house. If the courtyard was shared by a few families the cooks would sing and talk while they squatted at the clay ovens and the grinding stones.

This mud brick city gate was dug out of a hillside at Dan in Northern Israel. Maybe Abraham, Sarah, and their family walked through it forty centuries ago. The town of Dan was on the road leading into the Land of Israel. Tourists and archaeologists walk through the gate today. PHOTO COURTESY OF DOV GUBITCH

A City Mansion

Rich people lived in large houses made of wood and stone. Their plaster walls were often brightly painted or paneled with fine wood. The furniture was decorated with carved ivory and thin layers of gold. Many fancy houses were built around a cool courtyard filled with trees and flowers. The prophet Jeremiah scolded rich people for building large houses while they were stealing from the workmen. He said, "He builds his rooms with injustice and uses his neighbor's work without paying him."

A Poor City Home

Poor families sometimes lived in one or two rooms cut into the thick wall that surrounded the city. Rahab, the woman who helped the Israelites to conquer the city of Jericho, lived in the wall of the city. Other small homes were squeezed together along narrow city streets. On hot summer nights everyone crowded onto the roofs to sleep where it

was cooler. And on cold winter nights the family's chickens and goats were brought in to help warm the house.

Time to Go

Your muscles must be as creaky as Yavin's chariot wheels (Forgot Yavin? Look for him in Chapter Three). It's not easy to sleep on a straw mat, plow a field, carry jugs of water, and more. And maybe you're tired of goat cheese, barley bread, olives, and figs for breakfast, lunch, and supper. But wait—don't go home yet. A big holiday is coming. There'll be feasting, dancing, and singing. If Abigail and Ehud's family lived at the time of Solomon's Temple they'll take you to see the bright lights of Jerusalem. Move on to Chapter Seven and celebrate.

Two Bible Recipes

Jacob's Irresistible Lentil Soup

Jacob's older brother Esau loved lentil soup. One day when Esau came home from hunting he was very, very hungry. He almost fainted when he smelled his brother Jacob's soup cooking. "For a bowl of soup I'll sell you my birthright," he cried. "Done!" said Jacob. He ladled out the soup and won Esau's birthright—the right of the older brother to inherit all of their father Isaac's property and power.

To make lentil soup for five or six hungry hunters you will need:

3/4 cup of dried lentils
5 cups of water
1 large onion, peeled
1/2 tsp. salt
2 carrots
1 stalk of celery
1/2 cup uncooked elbow macaroni
pepper, basil, or other seasonings to taste
soup pot, 3 quart size
measuring cup
cutting board
knife
slotted spoon

1. Rinse the lentils. Let them soak in the water in the pot overnight.
2. Slice the peeled onion halfway through as shown. Add it to the soaked lentils.
3. Bring the water, lentils, and onion to a boil and cook at low flame for about an hour or until the lentils are soft.
4. Dice the carrots and celery as shown, add the vegetables, seasoning, and macaroni to the soup. Bring the soup to a boil, then cook at low flame for about 20 minutes or until the vegetables and macaroni are soft. Add water while cooking if the soup is too thick.
5. Take out the onion with the slotted spoon.

Serve hot with grated cheese and/or crumbled matzah.

Date Patties

Date palm trees grow in the Jordan Valley and other warm parts of Israel. Ancient Israelis ate fresh dates and also dried their dates in the sun to be used later. Try this recipe for a dried date snack. It makes about 20 patties.

You will need:

1/2 cup of shelled walnuts
1/2 pound of dried dates with the pits removed (about 24 dates)
1/4 cup of flour
3 tablespoons of butter
measuring cup
knife
cutting board
chopping knife and wood chopping bowl or food processor
tablespoon
frying pan
spatula

1. Chop the walnuts and dates in the wooden bowl or grind coarsely in the food processor.
2. Add the flour and mix.
3. Melt the 3 tablespoons of butter in the frying pan at low heat. Watch it—butter burns quickly! Add 1 1/2 tablespoons of melted butter to the date mixture.
4. Mix and squeeze the date mixture till it forms a ball. Place the ball on the cutting board and roll it to a roll about 1 1/2 or 2 inches round.

5. Refrigerate the roll for a least an hour—that makes it easier to cut.
6. Slice the roll into 1/4 inch thick patties.
7. Fry in the pan with the remaining melted butter at low heat for about 2 minutes on each side.

7 *Holidays in the Bible*

Holidays and Holier Days

A Jewish holiday is a Jewish holiday is a Jewish holiday. Right? Wrong! There are holidays and there are holier holidays. The holier holidays are the days that the Torah set aside for rest and prayer and for bringing gifts to God. Shabbat which comes each week is the holiday that the Torah mentions most often. In one of the Ten Commandments, God ordered Jews to rest from all their work on Shabbat. The Torah also calls on Jews to observe Rosh Hashanah, Yom Kippur, Sukkot, Passover, and Shavuot. Though the story of Purim is told in the Bible—in the Book of Esther—it was not celebrated as a holiday during Bible times.

Are you wondering what happened to Hanukkah and other holidays? They're important. But they only became important after the Bible was written. Kids in Bible times didn't light Hanukkah candles, eat potato pancakes and jelly donuts, and get presents. They didn't parade around the synagogue following the Torah on Simhat Torah. But what a great time they had at Sukkot, Passover, and Shavuot! Sukkot was the biggest holiday of the year because it came in the fall right after the big harvest.

Fun and Feasts and Thank You's to God

"Avi, help your brothers with the winnowing." (Winnowing means separating wheat husks from grain.)

"Sarah, help Grandma pack the dried figs."

"Squeeze the cheese."

"Collect the eggs and then bring a jug of water."

"Hurry! Hurry!"

"Orders! All the time orders!" the children must have grumbled. But they hurried. Everyone in the family worked from dawn to sunset in the last weeks of the summer. Stalks of grain had to be gathered, chopped up, and then tossed into the air with a pitchfork. The wind blew away the light husks and leaves, and the heavy grain fell to the ground. Then the grain was poured into huge jars and stored for the winter. With itchy husks still sticking in their hair the kids went on to pack dried figs and raisins into baskets. Or to pound grain into flour. Or to squeeze green-gold oil out of the olives. Or to pick the last cucumbers, watermelons, or pomegranates. The great harvest holiday of Sukkot was only a few days away.

When the hard work was finally done there was time for the fun jobs. The kids decorated the wagons with flowers and leaves. They even made necklaces of flowers for the donkeys and oxen who would pull the wagons. The grown-ups packed food and gifts for the Temple. Then the little kids and old people climbed into the wagon and onto the donkeys. Everyone else walked alongside. They were on their way to Jerusalem, the home of the Holy Temple!

"I see it! I see it!"

"I saw it first!"

The kids pointed and yelled as they came around a turn in the path and saw the golden Temple shimmering on its mountain top. The road grew wider and became more crowded. Jews were coming to Jerusalem from all corners of the land. Cousins, uncles, aunts, and old friends met and hugged and walked happily together. By the time they reached the gate of the city it was evening. But a full moon lit the city wall and silvered the olive trees at the foot of the wall. There was plenty of light to unload the donkeys and put up a shelter or a sukkah. The kids curled up on their mats to sleep. But who could sleep? The smoke of the campfire tickled their noses, and they shivered at the unfamiliar city noises. Chariot wheels were pounding through the city streets, people were shouting, and Israelite soldiers were marching back and forth to change the guard at the gate.

text continued on page 74

So That's Where It Comes From!
Jewish Holidays

"These are the times for holy gatherings," says the Torah, the Five Books of Moses. The Torah tells about these holy gatherings in many chapters. Rosh Hodesh, the festival of the new moon, is described in the Book of Numbers with these words: "and in the beginning of your months you shall offer a burnt offering to the Lord."

The Book of Leviticus also gives holiday instructions. Here they are, a little shortened:

Shabbat—God spoke to Moses and said, "These are the times I have chosen for holy gatherings. Six days you shall work, but the seventh day is a rest day and a day of holy meeting."

Passover—These are the chosen times of the Lord. . . . In the first month, on the fourteenth day . . . is the Lord's Passover. . . . Seven days you shall eat unleavened bread, matzah. On the first day you shall have a holy gathering, . . . and on the seventh day . . . you will bring a bundle of the first fruit of your harvest (the omer) to the priest.

Shavuot—You shall count (from the first day of Passover) seven weeks, . . . and you shall bring a new offering to the Lord (two loaves of bread). There shall be a holy gathering and you shall do no work.

Rosh Hashanah—The first day of the seventh month shall be a solemn day of rest, a holy gathering which is called with the blowing of horns. . . .

Yom Kippur—The tenth day of the seventh month is the day of atonement. . . . It shall be for you a sabbath of solemn rest and you will afflict your souls.

Sukkot—On the fifteenth day of the seventh month when you have gathered the fruits of the land you shall keep the feast of the Lord for seven days. . . . On the first day you shall take the fruit of the trees (etrog), branches of palm trees, of thick trees and of willows . . . you shall live in booths (sukkot) for seven days . . . so that you may know that I made the children of Israel live in booths when I brought them out of Egypt.

Shemini Atseret—The eighth day shall be a holy gathering for you.

Did you notice that the Book of Leviticus starts counting the months of the year at Passover? That makes Passover come on the first month, and Rosh Hashanah, Yom Kippur, and Sukkot come out in the seventh month of the year.

Making Music at the Temple

When the Levites sang and the priests sounded the trumpets the glory of the Lord filled the House of God.

–SECOND BOOK OF CHRONICLES 5:12-14

After the Temple was destroyed by the Romans the music making ended. "How can we play musical instruments when our Temple is gone?" said the rabbis. For the next 1800 years only singing was heard in synagogues. But in the mid-1800s Reform Jews brought organs into their synagogues. Today you may hear pianos, guitars, or organs at some synagogue services. At others you'll hear only the voices of the cantor and the worshippers.

trumpet
(gold or silver)

water whistle

small lyre
(gut and wood)

rattles
(pottery, wood, or metal)

timbrel or drum
(wood and skin)

shofar
(ram's horn)

flute or recorder
(reed)

panpipe
(reed)

Illustrations are drawn from reconstructed Bible instruments at the Haifa Museum in Israel.

> Raise a child in the way he or she should go and when the child grows up he or she will not depart from it.
>
> PROVERBS 22:6

In the morning bright fingers of sunlight poked into the sukkah. They had time for a cold, splashing wash-up at the spring, a breakfast of cheese and pita bread, and then, clutching leafy branches, they walked through the city gate into Jerusalem. The kids held each other's hands and grabbed their parents' robes. There were so many people brushing past them. So many voices calling out and animals bleating and baa-ing. Their father pulled along two goats and the children held baskets of bread, grapes, and vegetables. These were the family's gifts to God and to the Temple priests. The priests would give part of the meat back to the family. And each evening of the holiday they would roast meat over their campfire and feast. It was only on holidays that they could afford to eat meat.

The family climbed the steps leading to the Temple courtyards. At the top the wide, sunny courtyard was like a rolling, green sea. Everyone was carrying golden etrogim and branches of willow, palm, or other trees to celebrate the Sukkot holiday. Far ahead the children could see a great column of black smoke. It was rising from the top of the tall altar. So tall, thought the kids, that if three of us stood on top of each other we wouldn't reach the top. The priests climbed a ramp to the top where they prepared sacrifices to God.

The beat of the drums, jingle of tambourines, and shrill piping of whistles and flutes sounded over the voices of the people. Standing on tiptoes the children could see the Levites, the Temple musicians, wearing white robes. They were lined up on each side of the altar playing their instruments and singing songs of praise to God. But off to one side they

heard an angry, hoarse voice. They moved toward it and saw a tall, bony man in a dusty, brown robe. He was pounding his stick on the pavement and shouting, "God doesn't want your sacrifices and your solemn gatherings. You get drunk on wine at your festivals and you forget God's laws! God will stop the rain and let your fields dry out. God will punish the Hebrew people for their sins. . . . "

Quickly the father pulled his family away. "The man is a troublemaker," he said indignantly. "We're doing what God wants. We came to the Temple and brought two fat goats for the Lord. What more can we do? Someone should shut him up! He'll bring bad luck!"

"He's a prophet," said the mother. "Maybe God sent him to warn us."

"A troublemaker!" the father insisted. The children looked fearfully at the troublemaker-prophet. Was he right? Would God really stop the rain?

The music grew louder. It drew them back to the altar. They skipped to the beat of the drums and stood on tiptoes to see over the people in front. A huge, bronze basin stood beside the altar. It was three times as big as the well in their village, and it was held on the backs of twelve oxen made of metal. The priests climbed down from the smoking altar to wash their hands in the basin. The Levite musician's voices rang out. Their prayers mixed with the rippling lyres and harps and swelled and sank like the waves of Lake Kinneret. Whistles shrilled, flutes trilled, and clay drums thumped. "The music is going right up to God's ears," the children whispered. "It will make God happy and then God will listen to our prayers." They sang out loud along with the Levites.

Later, around the supper campfires, the grown-ups sang and the kids played hide and seek in the cool evening air. Jugs of wine were passed around. Happy dancers swayed and wiggled as they circled the fire. And

others sat together and talked. They made matches between sons and daughters, planned weddings, traded crops, and sold land.

Sukkot was the happiest, busiest time of the year. On the long walk home at the end of the holiday everyone was tired and satisfied. Soon the first autumn rains will fall, they thought, and we'll have all winter to do quiet work. I'll weave cloth for new robes—the kids are growing right out of their old ones, thought the mother. I'll ask Oved the potter to make two new jars for oil, thought the father. But a few of the pilgrims remembered the prophet in the dusty robe and wondered, "Is God really angry at us? Will the rain fall?"

More Holidays of the Bible

Passover in early spring and Shavuot in late spring were pilgrimage holidays like Sukkot. At Passover time the early barley was ripening in the fields and the grapevines were flowering. Jews brought a first sheaf or bundle of their ripe barley to the Temple. It was called the omer. Seven weeks later, at Shavuot, after counting fifty days of the omer and watching their first fruits ripen, they brought loaves of fine wheat bread and baskets of new fruit to the Temple.

"Thank you, God, for the rain and the sun and the harvest of grain and fruit," they sang along with the Levites. "And spread Your shelter of peace over us. Amen."

From Then to Now

Before King Solomon built the First Temple in Jerusalem the Israelites worshipped at the shrine of Shiloh. That's where little Samuel served God. (You'll find his story in Chapter Five.) They also brought sacrifices to hilltop altars near their homes. After Solomon built the Temple, Israelites came to Jerusalem to worship at God's house. Most of them were farmers and they prayed for rain or dew or good crops. Then they had barbecues, danced, sang, and went sight-seeing in the big city. The celebrations may've gotten wild because Isaiah the prophet complained that people got drunk at Sukkot. And another prophet, Amos, said they got too rowdy.

In 586 B.C.E. the Temple was destroyed. Many Jews were dragged off

text continued on page 78

A Year of Modern Jewish Holidays

Can you tell how many of these holidays began in the days of the Bible?

Shabbat, the day of rest, comes each week.

Rosh Hodesh is celebrated at the beginning of each month.

Because Hebrew months follow the moon's cycle and secular months follow the sun's cycle they line up with each other differently each year. The line-up shown on the chart changes each year.

to Babylonia as captives. They could no longer offer sacrifices in the Temple. They could only offer their prayers. Some scholars believe that the first synagogues were founded in exile in Babylonia. The exiles would gather in the synagogues to observe Shabbat and celebrate festivals.

When many Jews returned from Babylonia to the Land of Israel they rebuilt the Temple and the walls around Jerusalem. On festivals they came to the Temple where the priests conducted sacrifices and colorful ceremonies. Jews from faraway lands came back to Jerusalem at holiday times to take part in Temple services. But even in the Land of Israel the synagogues continued to be centers of study and prayer where each worshipper spoke directly to God.

Simhat Torah celebration. ISRAELI CONSULATE

Then, in 70 C.E. the second Temple was destroyed by the armies of Rome. A few years later the Jews lost not only their Temple but also the land under their feet. The Romans forced many of them to leave their beloved homes, farms, olive groves, and vineyards and go to foreign lands. If there were no more farms how could there be farmer's holidays?

Wise leaders reminded the people of other meanings for each holiday. Sukkot helped the Jews to remember their wandering in the desert after God had brought them out of Egypt. Passover was the story of their struggle to free themselves from slavery. And Shavuot celebrated the day that God gave the Torah to the Jewish people at Mount Sinai. Rosh Hashanah became the thought-filled beginning of the new year. Yom Kippur was a solemn fast day. And Hanukkah, Purim, and other holidays soon came along to brighten the months. Slowly the holidays of the Jewish year began to look like the Jewish holidays we know today. And they were celebrated in the homes and synagogues of each Jewish community.

A Re-Birth Day

A thousand years ago the chief rabbi in Babylonia added a new celebration to the week-long holiday of Sukkot, which ends with Shemini Atseret. The new celebration was called Simhat Torah, rejoicing in the Torah. Reading the Torah had always been part of the synagogue service. A section of the Torah called *parashat hashavuah* was read each week. On the new holiday of Simhat Torah it became the custom to finish reading the Torah scroll and immediately to start at the beginning again. Ever since, for one thousand years, Jews have read the Torah in the synagogue from Simhat Torah to Simhat Torah.

By Simhat Torah the scroll has been rolled so far that one pole holds a very thick part of the scroll and the other pole a very thin part. On the morning of Simhat Torah the last section of the scroll is read. Then all the Torah's are taken out of the ark. In a happy, singing parade they are carried around the synagogue. They circle around at least seven times. The kids run and skip and march along too, waving flags, shouting, and singing. Noise is okay at Simhat Torah because it's a party.

When the parade is finished all the Torahs except one are put back into the ark. The remaining Torah is rolled backward from the second pole to the first, back to the very beginning. And then the Torah has a rebirth. Its new birthday year begins as the reader chants the first line of the First Book of Moses, "In the beginning God created the heaven and the earth . . . "

Make a Party for the Bible on Simhat Torah

Make a Ten Commandments cake and prepare punch or juice to drink.
Make paper chain decorations for the *sukkah* or party room.
Make flags and have a contest with prizes for the flag that's funniest, that tells the most about the holiday, that's most colorful, most imaginative, and even the wildest and silliest. After all, it is a party.
Play "Who Am I?" using the names of Bible people.

Here's how:

Ten Commandments Cake

You will need:

> the batter of any layer cake recipe (a cake mix is okay)
> one cup of any flavor icing
> one tablespoon of shortening and 2 tablespoons of flour to grease and
> > sprinkle pans
> 1/2 cup chocolate chips, nuts, M & Ms, gum drops, or anything else
> > you like to decorate the cake and mark the commandments

one 8 inch round layer cake pan
one 8 inch square pan
large bowl for batter
small bowl for icing
mixing spoons
toothpick
knife to cut cake
cardboard, at least 10 by 18 inches, covered with aluminum foil

Follow these steps:

1. Grease the two baking pans. Sprinkle them lightly with flour.
2. Heat the oven to 350°.
3. Mix the batter for any layer cake recipe.
4. Pour half of the batter into the round cake pan. Pour the other half into the square pan.
5. Bake until a toothpick poked into the middle of the batter comes out dry (about 20 minutes).
6. Let the cakes cool. Cut each cake in half as shown.
7. Take them out of the pans. Place them on the cardboard as shown.
8. Ice the cake. Decorate with chocolate chips, nuts, raisins, whatever, and mark the commandments as shown.

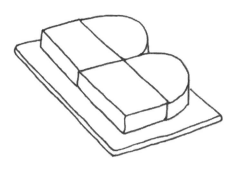

Paper Chains

1. Cut colored paper into long strips about 4 inches wide. You can use newspaper comic strips, bright wrapping paper, or construction paper.
2. Fold the strips every 2 inches as shown.

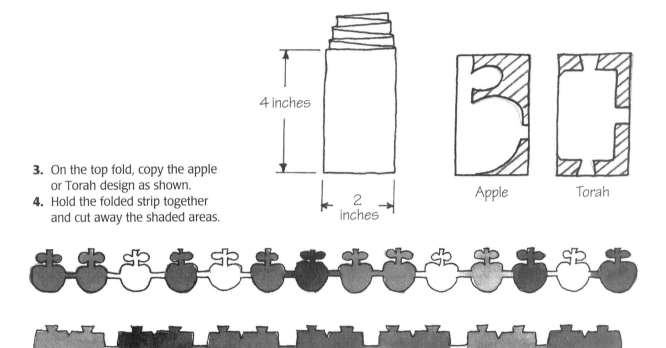

3. On the top fold, copy the apple or Torah design as shown.

4. Hold the folded strip together and cut away the shaded areas.

Flags

The usual designs on Simhat Torah flags are Jewish stars, shofar or menorah shapes, Torah shapes, and Ten Commandment shapes.

Prepare glue, stapler, scissors, colored paper, glitter, colored markers or crayons, yarn, sticks or dowels for mounting the flags, . . . and anything else you can think of. Decorate your flag and staple it to the stick or dowel.

Who Am I ?????

Write the name of a well-known Bible person on a card. Tape the card to the back of one player.

All the other players can see the name. The player wearing the card asks anyone in the circle questions that can be answered with a "yes" or a "no" until the player guesses who he or she is. You may want to allow up to ten questions.

Examples: Did I love lentil soup? Did I stutter? Did I build the First Temple?

Answers: Esau. Moses. Solomon.

8 After the Bible—More and More Books of Torah

Law

The Jewish people lost their second golden Temple in 70 C.E. It was destroyed by the armies of Rome. Suddenly there was no more music and dancing, no more sacrificing to God and happy, holiday gatherings in the Temple courtyards. Only sooty, black stones were left on the torn-up hilltop. Many people were killed or driven out of the land. Those that remained were a small, weak group. What was left for the Jewish people? What could hold them together? A special book called the Talmud, which was put together five hundred years after the Temple was destroyed, tells us that it was the law that kept the Jews together. As Jews studied the law and stories of the Bible they felt that God was with them. God cared about them. And some day God would bring them home to the Promised Land. Here's how the Talmud describes the passing of the law from generation to generation:

> Moses received the Law at Mount Sinai
> And handed it to Joshua,
> Joshua to the elders (the judges),
> The elders to the prophets,
> And the prophets to the men of the Great Assembly.
> *—FROM THE "SAYINGS OF THE FATHERS," TALMUD*

The Talmud is written in many volumes. It is so big that it is called the Sea of Talmud. Learning to swim through those centuries of ideas takes hard study. Today computers are life-savers in finding answers in the Talmud. Rabbi Judah never had it this good!

The Great Assembly

During the days when the Second Temple still stood shining on its hill-top the men of the Great Assembly began to build a different kind of Temple inside the heart of each Jew. The Great Assembly was a gathering of judges and teachers of Torah in Judea. They discussed and explained the Torah's laws and tried to make them part of people's daily lives. When the Second Temple was destroyed their teachings and the teaching of later scholars became the lifeline that tied the Jews to their God and to each other.

"We must study the Torah again and again. It contains everything," said the scholars. After a day of work in the fields or workshops they would meet in the cool evening, slap at mosquitos, and search the Torah for answers. Hillel, Shammai, Akiva, and other rabbis would read a line

Moses received the Law at Mount Sinai.

of Torah and then explain it. For instance, they found a message of care and kindness to animals in these short sentences in Deuteronomy 11:15.

> I will give grass in the field for your cattle
> And you will eat and be satisfied.

Rabbi Judah explained, "God promised grass for the cattle *before* God promised that the cattle owner would eat. That means it's forbidden for people to eat before they have fed their animals."

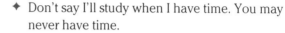

The Talmud states that there were 394 synagogues in Jerusalem alone while the Second Temple was still standing.

Though these scholars talked and talked, sometimes all night long, they could say a lot in very few words. See if you understand these proverbs from the Sayings of the Fathers in the Talmud.

- ✦ If I don't take care of myself—who will take care of me? But if I care only about myself—what good am I? And if not now—when?
- ✦ Don't keep yourself apart from the people around you.
- ✦ Don't judge someone else until you are in his or her place.
- ✦ Don't say I'll study when I have time. You may never have time.
- ✦ It's better to be a tail among lions than a head among foxes.

The most patient, kindest teacher in the Great Assembly was Rabbi Hillel. One day a non-Jew came to him and said, "I want to become a Jew, but only if you can teach me the whole Torah while I stand on one foot." Instead of getting angry at the man's *hutzpah*, or "impudence," Hillel answered, "It's very simple. Don't do anything to your neighbor that you would hate to have someone do to you. That is the whole Torah. All the rest is explanation or commentary. Now go and learn it."

The Mishnah

The Bible or Tanakh had been written on scrolls made of parchment, animal skin. It was called the "Written" Torah. After the Torah was completed the scholars of the Great Assembly continued to teach the law. But their teachings weren't written down—they were spoken. Year after year, from grandparents to grandchildren, from teachers to students, the teachings were told and retold. They were called "Oral" Torah. As the Oral Torah grew longer it got harder to remember. At last in 200 C.E. Rabbi Judah ha-Nasi gathered the oral teachings into a book. It was called the Mishnah. At about the same time some of the verses and prayers from the Written Torah were collected to form a service for daily prayer. Since the Jews couldn't bring their prayers and sacrifices to God at the Temple they would bring their prayers and hopes to a synagogue and pray together.

Holy Arithmetic:
Mishnah + Gemarah = Talmud

Rabbi Judah must have sighed with relief and taken a long nap when he finished putting together the Mishnah. But before the ink was dry the rabbis were already adding explanations to the Torah and Mishnah. One group of rabbis met and debated in central and northern Israel. The other group met in Babylonia. They discussed laws of marriage and divorce, astronomy, mathematics, holidays, cures for fever, and a million other subjects. It was a 600 to 700 year long conversation. The conversation and study ended for the Israeli rabbis in about 400 C.E. when they combined the Mishnah with their book of deliberations, called the Gemarah. The entire work was called the Jerusalem Talmud. The Babylonian rabbis thought and talked for another 100 years and finally assembled their Gemarah and the Mishnah into the Babylonian Talmud. Over the centuries the Babylonian Talmud has been used more widely than the Jerusalem Talmud because later rabbis wrote more comments about its laws and debates.

After the Jews were driven out of Jerusalem by the Romans many Jewish scholars met again on the round, green hills of northern Israel. In towns like Tzippori and Bet Shearim they continued studying and explaining the Torah. Rabbi Judah ha-Nasi, who put together the Mishnah, lived here in Tzippori.

Oral Torah, Written Torah— What's the Difference?

Talmud writers cared a lot about the difference between Oral and Written Torah. This story tells how they explained it:

> A king had two favorite servants. He gave each of them a basket of wheat and a bundle of flax, a tall grass that's used to make cloth. The wise ser-

vant took the flax and spun a cloth. He took the wheat and made
flour. He kneaded and baked the flour into bread. Then he put the
bread on the table and covered it with the cloth, ready for the king.
The foolish servant did nothing. After a few days the king returned
from a journey and said to the servants, "My sons, bring me what I
gave you." The wise servant brought the bread covered with the
cloth. The foolish servant brought only the basket of wheat with the
flax on top. He was disgraced!

The scholars explain, "When the Holy One, of Blessing, gave the
Torah to Israel it was given only in the form of wheat, for us to make flour
and bread. And in the form of flax, for us to make cloth."

You and I are not Talmud scholars so I'll tell you what I think the
story means. See if you agree:

The words of the Tanakh or Bible, the Written Torah, are like hard
grains of wheat and bundles of flax. We can't eat hard grains of wheat or
wear bundles of flax. In the same way, we often can't understand and
apply the wise, concise words of the Written Torah exactly as we read
them.

People have to grind the wheat to make the bread to eat. And they
have to clean and spin the flax to make cloth for clothing. In the same
way, people have to think about the words of the Written Torah, explain
and interpret them for each other, and learn how to put the teachings
into action in their daily lives.

These explanations and interpretations based on the words of the
Written Torah are called Oral Torah.

*What's inside a mezuzzah,
the small container nailed to
the door frame of a Jewish
home? Hand-written words
from the Bible that remind
Jews to love God and obey
God's laws. The exact words
are in the Torah's Book of
Deuteronomy 6:4–9 and
11:13–21.*

*First Torah, Then Talmud,
Then More*

Even after the Talmud was finished the Oral Torah kept growing.
Teachers explained Torah with stories like the story of Baby Moses and
the glowing charcoal at the end of Chapter Five. And they used lessons
called midrash to teach people how to behave. One midrash comments
on the Bible's story of Noah who built an ark, gathered pairs of all living
things, and floated on the flood waters for forty days. It's a good story,
but the midrash adds a lesson. It tells that Noah worked very hard caring
for all the animals. When he came out onto dry land he planted a vine-

yard. Then he made wine from the grapes and got very drunk. "What happened when he got drunk?" asked the rabbis. Here's their disapproving answer: "Noah learned too much from the animals on the ark. When he began drinking he started off bleating like a lamb. Soon he began to roar like a lion. And he ended up acting like a monkey."

Century after century people kept adding ideas and comments to the Torah stories. Maimonides in Egypt in the twelfth century and Rashi in France in the eleventh century were the most famous commentators. Rashi's ideas are printed in a special alphabet in tiny type on the pages of many modern books of Torah and Talmud. In thirteenth-century Spain a book named the Zohar appeared. It tried to explain the nature of God. In the 1500s Joseph Caro wrote the Shulhan Arukh, the "Prepared Table," which gave rules to show people how to follow the ideas of the Torah and Talmud. From the time they got up in the morning until they went to sleep at night there were rules to follow. Very observant Jews still live by the rules of the Shulhan Arukh. At about the same time other rabbis wrote books on Kabbalah (also spelled Cabala), based on the Zohar, which searched for ways to bring the Messiah to earth.

A Torah-Bible Mishmash

Bible or Tanakh means the Five Books of Moses, the Book of Prophets, and the Book of Writings. Torah means the Five Books of Moses, which are written in the Torah scroll. Torah also means the many writings over the centuries that are based on the Torah such as the Talmud, responsa, prayer book, commentaries, Kabbalah, etc. Therefore—the very first book of Judaism is the Torah, and all the other writings of the Jewish religion are Torah too!

Is that clear? No? Maybe this diagram will help explain it. Torah is like a tree with the Five Books of Moses as its roots and trunk.

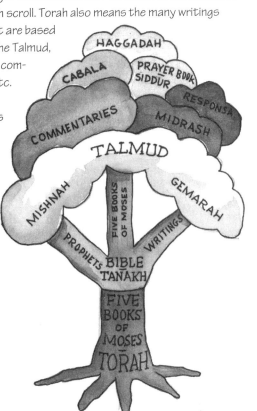

Throughout Jewish history until today there have been 250,000 responsa exchanged between questioners and answering rabbis. Bar Ilan University in Israel has produced a CD-ROM which contains thousands of responsa.

Responsa

Responsa, answers, are another kind of Oral Torah. People would ask questions of their rabbi. Questions such as: may a father forbid his son to go and live in the Holy Land? Or: may matzah made by machine be used on Passover? Sometimes the rabbi couldn't answer the question. So he would send it on to a more learned rabbi. The question might have to travel a long way by camel caravan, donkey, or sailing ship. When it reached the wise teacher he would search the Torah for guidance. Then he would send his answer on the long trip back. Months or even years later the answer would finally reach the questioner.

text continued on page 90

Oif'n Pripitchek—On the Hearth

Parents and teachers sang this Yiddish song for many years. It tells how a child begins to study Torah. Artist Saul Raskin drew the picture on the opposite page to illustrate the song.

> On the hearth
> A small fire burns
> And the house is warm.
> And the teacher teaches little boys
> The alef-bet to form.
>
> Remember children,
> Remember dear ones,
> What you study for.
> Say again and once again
> *Kometz* [ָ], *alef* [א]—*aww* [אָ]

From the moment a child was born Torah became part of his life. At the *brit* ceremony baby boys became partners to Abraham's agreement with God. After the *brit* the family and guests called out, "May he study Torah and get married and do good deeds. Mazel tov!" Only three years later little boys got their first haircut, were wrapped in a *tallit*, and were carried to school to begin their studies.

In the twelfth century the terrified Jews of Yemen sent a painful question to Maimonides in Egypt. "Our ruler has forced us to become Muslims," they wrote. "If we had not converted he would have killed us. What can we do now?" Maimonides wrote back and comforted them. "In the past Jews have been forced to pretend to accept other religions," he wrote, "but in the end Judaism always won out. Don't be afraid. Israel will outlive its persecutors."

Responsa are still being written. Today they go by fax or e-mail rather than on the backs of camels or donkeys. But the questions are just as hard to answer. Think of how you might answer the following:

✦ Three people need a heart transplant immediately. Only one heart has been found. Who should decide which person will get the heart? On what basis should the decision be made?

✦ Many Jews in Israel live on land that was promised to Israel in the Bible. But some of the land is outside the borders that the United Nations set for the modern State of Israel. Should the Israelis give back some of the Promised Land in the hope of making peace with their neighbors?

✦ A sheep has been cloned, an exact copy was made, from the genes of another sheep. Should other animals be cloned—perhaps to provide more milk or meat? Should human beings be cloned—perhaps to provide special skills or brain power?

The word Torah doesn't mean "law." It means "teaching." It comes from the same root as the Hebrew word morah, which means "teacher."

From Hand to Hand

Remember, at the beginning of the chapter you read the words of the Talmud which said that the law was given to Moses, who passed it to Joshua, who passed it to the judges or elders, who passed it to the prophets, . . . and the prophets passed it to the scholars of the Great Assembly.

What happened next?

From the time of the Great Assembly, almost 2,000 years ago, until today Jews all over the world have lived with and added to the Oral Torah. So we are the next step—we Jews of today. The law was handed from the scholars of the Great Assembly to us, the Jewish people. From hand to hand. From the hand of Moses in a direct line to you and me!

So That's Where It Comes From!
Jewish Customs That Grew from the Bible

Law or Custom	Some Places to Find It in the Bible
Separating dairy and meat foods and utensils	You shall not cook a kid, a baby goat, in its mother's milk. —Exodus 34:26, Deuteronomy 14:21
Meat must be drained and salted	You shall not eat the blood, for the blood is the life. —Genesis 9:3–4, Deuteronomy 12:23
Some kinds of meat and fish may be eaten Some may not be eaten	You may eat every animal which has a divided hoof and chews its cud. . . . of all that are in the waters, all that have fins and scales shall you eat. —Deuteronomy 14:6–10
Circumcision or *brit milah*—when a baby boy is eight days old he is circumcised	God said to Abraham, "This is my covenant which you shall keep . . . He (a child) that is eight days old shall be circumcised; . . . every male throughout your generations (shall be circumcised)." —Genesis 17:10–12
Laws for observing Shabbat	Remember the Shabbat day to keep it holy. Six days you shall work, but the seventh day is a Sabbath to God. In it you shall not do any work, neither you, nor your son, your daughter, your manservant, maidservant, cattle, nor the stranger who lives with you. —Exodus 20:8–10
Wearing a fringed prayer shawl with a blue thread while praying. Orthodox Jews also wear a *tallit katan*, "fringed vest," under their shirts	. . . have the Children of Israel make fringes on the corners of their garments . . . with a thread of blue . . . that you may look at it and remember all the commandments of the Lord. —Numbers 15:38–39
Pidyon ha-ben, or "redeeming the first-born". When a first-born boy is 30 days old the parents pay a sum of money to a Kohen, a descendant of the Temple priests, to symbolically free the baby from service in the Temple. It reminds Jews of the long-ago Temple.	All the first-born males from a month old . . . from the first-born of the children of Israel he (Moses) took the redemption money. —Numbers 3:43–50
Placing a *mezuzzah* on the door post and laying *tefillin*, "phylacteries". Observant Jews lay tefillin when they recite morning prayers except on Shabbat and holidays.	You shall bind them (the words which I command you) for a sign on your arm and for frontlets between your eyes (on your fore-head) and you shall write them upon the door posts of your house. —Deuteronomy 6:8–9

9 New Branches from the Torah

Start with the Yeast

Did you ever use yeast to make hallah? Remember how the yeast makes the dough bubble and grow until it reaches the top of the bowl? That was how the ideas of the Torah bubbled and grew as the rabbis and teachers found new ways to explain them. A bowl of yeast batter grows until it can make enough bread to feed a big family. The Torah was like a batter that made bread not only for the Jews but for millions of others in the human family.

About 2,000 years ago many non-Jewish people in the Middle East started to turn away from their old beliefs. They stopped praying to idols, to the sun and moon, and even to their kings and queens. There must be something or someone bigger, who sees and knows everything and who cares about us, they thought. From Jews who lived among them they heard of the one God who watches over all living things. That sounded good. But it wasn't exactly right for them. The Torah made too many

Shady Holy Places
Jews, Christians, and Muslims share many holy places in Israel. The tombs of Abraham, Sarah, and other Bible ancestors are in the city of Hebron. Rachel, Jacob's second wife, is buried near Bethlehem. Both Jews and Muslims come to the tombs to pray and to beg their great ancestors for help. Other holy places are found all over the country. They're easy to recognize because Israel isn't blessed with many big, old trees, and there are always tall trees growing around holy places, shading the visitors. This is a photo of the tomb of Rabbi Halafta. The black smudges on the wall were made by the smoke of candles that visitors lit in the rabbi's honor.

demands, such as circumcising baby boys and eating only kosher food. They wanted to change the religion just a little bit. So they used many of the ideas of the Torah as yeast in their own batter of religion. And out of that bubbling batter grew two new religions. The first was Christianity. The second, which came a few centuries later, was called Islam.

Christianity

In the last years before the Romans destroyed the Second Temple a young rabbi and teacher called Jesus wandered through the Galilee in northern Israel. He stopped and taught his own view of Torah to other Jews and to anyone who would listen. Jesus taught mostly about the gentle, loving side of God who takes care of even the poorest people just as God takes care of the birds of the air. He told his followers that God would forgive those who broke God's laws. Jesus taught, "Whatever you want people to do to you, so should you do to them. That is the most important law of all." A few years before, Hillel, the wise teacher of the Mishnah, used almost the same words. This simple message of love and

On a hill in Nazareth, Israel, stands the Church of the Annunciation. Christians believe that the angel Gabriel came to Mary at this site and told her that she would conceive and give birth to a son. He would be called Jesus, the son of the Highest. The New Testament tells that Jesus grew up in the town of Nazareth.

forgiveness made some Jews very happy. Maybe Jesus is the Messiah we've been waiting for, they thought. When Jesus came to Jerusalem one Passover his followers gathered around him and called him "Messiah."

"Messiah!" That was a word that raised the blood pressure of the Roman rulers of Jerusalem. "Messiah" means "anointed one," usually a king. The Roman rulers had already had enough trouble with other people who called themselves messiahs. Such people would gather a lot of unruly followers, block traffic on the roads and even try to overthrow the Roman

governor. To put down this new messiah the Romans brought in more soldiers, raised taxes, and pushed people around. That was bad for the Jews, so the Jewish leaders were unhappy about this messiah, too.

The Romans squashed the new messiah quickly. They arrested Jesus, had a trial, and executed him on a cross. But to their surprise that didn't end the story. It was only the beginning. The followers of Jesus still believed that he was the messiah and the son of God. They called him "Christ," which means messiah in Greek. And they were sure he hadn't died at all. "He came back to life after he was killed," they said. "And he will come back to save the world. We don't have to

SO THAT'S WHERE IT COMES FROM

So That's Where It Comes From!
The Messiah

Many Jews believe that God will some day send a messiah who will bring God's kingdom to the earth. Christians also believe in a messiah, but they believe that the messiah has already come and that he is Jesus Christ. They believe that Jesus will come back again.

In legends the Messiah will come jogging along on a white donkey, blowing a shofar, and waking everyone to tell them the good news. Yet the Bible only hints at the coming of the Messiah. Later books like the Talmud and writings on Kabbalah describe the Messiah as a real being who is waiting anxiously for the day on which the Jews will be worthy of receiving him.

Here are two examples of the Bible's hints:

A shoot will grow from [the trunk of] the tree of Jesse [King David's father], and a branch will grow out of his roots and the spirit of the Lord will rest on him . . . and he shall judge the poor with righteousness and will be fair to the humblest people. [At that time] the wolf shall live with the lamb and the leopard shall lie down with the young goat and a little child shall lead them. They shall not hurt or destroy in all my holy mountain.

—ISAIAH 11:1–9

You are small [town of] Bethlehem [birthplace of David and Jesus] yet the one who is to be ruler of Israel will come out of you. He comes from an ancient time, from the days of old.

—MICAH 5:1

Kfar Nahum is the name of a fishing village that once stood on the shore of Lake Kinneret in Israel. The millstone in this photo, stone tools, and the walls of an ancient synagogue were found here. In the synagogue of Kfar Nahum, 2,000 years ago, Jesus is said to have proclaimed, "Repent because the kingdom of God is at hand."

worry about being poor or oppressed in this world. Jesus will save us and bring us into heaven."

At first, most of the followers of Jesus were Jews and they continued to believe in the laws of the Torah. But most other Jews would not believe that Jesus was the Messiah and would not accept his follower's ideas. After a while the leaders of the new religion began to drop some Biblical laws. They stopped circumcising males and they no longer ate only kosher food or observed Shabbat strictly. Soon they moved Shabbat from Saturday to Sunday to make it different from the Jewish day of rest. Without the Torah's strict laws it was easier for a non-Jew to accept the new religion. Christianity quickly spread among non-Jews in the Roman empire.

About 300 years after Jesus had been executed the Roman emperor himself became a Christian and the religion spread through all the lands he ruled.

Christian leaders gathered the teachings of Jesus into a book called the New Testament. By that time Judaism and Christianity had become completely separate religions. But many Christians read (and still read) the Hebrew Bible. They think of the Hebrew Bible as the Old Testament on which their New Testament is based.

Only 600 years after Jesus' lifetime another religion grew out of the Torah. It swept the Middle East and much of Europe, Asia, and Africa. Like Christianity it's still with us today. The religion is called Islam.

At the worst times in their lives many Jews found comfort in their belief in the messiah. During World War Two when Jews were trapped in Nazi death camps they sang "Ani maamin." The words of the song mean "I believe, with all my faith, in the coming of the Messiah."

The Dome of the Rock

Al-Aksa and Dome of the Rock mosques are Muslim houses of worship built on the Temple Mount in Jerusalem. They were built here because the Koran tells that Mohammed flew up to heaven in a night journey from this very hilltop. Many years earlier the First and Second Temples had stood here. And even earlier the Bible tells us that Abraham brought his son Isaac here, to Mount Moriah, as a sacrifice to God. And . . . long, long before Isaac's scary climb a legend tells us that God took earth from Mount Moriah to shape the body of Adam, the first human being. That's a heavy load of history and holiness for one little hill to carry. PHOTO COURTESY OF ED TOBEN

Islam

One starry night, 600 years after Jesus had lived, an Arab merchant from the town of Mecca went out to the desert to sit alone and think. Suddenly a voice called out and startled him. The Muslim Bible, the Koran, tells us that it was the voice of the angel Gabriel. The angel gave the merchant, Mohammed, the rules and ideas of a new religion. In the new religion there is only one god. His name is Allah and Mohammed is his prophet. There is a day of judgment when people will be judged for their deeds. And there is a paradise and a hell where human beings will be rewarded or punished. Islam, the name of the new religion, means submitting to Allah's will.

Mohammed told everyone in Mecca about his vision. But instead of being cheered he got loud boos. People in Mecca believed in lots of gods. There were 300 gods in the local temple. One of them was called Allah. The Meccans even worshipped a black meteorite which had fallen from heaven. Why should they drop all the other gods and accept only Allah? Besides, they had heard Mohammed's ideas before. Many of them were like the laws and stories of the Torah and the Christian New

text continued on page 98

A Story: How to Live Happily Ever After
—adapted from *Legends of Judea and Samaria by Zev Vilnay*

Muslims, Jews, and Christians often lived peacefully together in the Land of Israel. But, as this story shows, it took careful planning to keep everyone happy.

Three boyfriends wanted to marry the beautiful princess of Caesarea, a city on the coast of Israel. One was Muslim, one Jewish, and one Christian. She liked each one of them so much that she couldn't choose between them. Her father, the king, warned her, "Whichever one you choose will anger the believers in the other two religions in our city. Instead of choosing, set the men to do an important task. The one who completes the task can become your husband."

"Sounds good," said the princess. "What task?"

"Caesarea doesn't have good water. We need to build aqueducts, water carriers, to bring fresh water from the hills to the city. Ask each young man to build an aqueduct. Then marry the one who finishes first."

The princess agreed. Each of her boyfriends eagerly started building. But it was hard, hot work. After a while one young man got tired and stopped. Awhile later the second boyfriend found that his aqueduct was far behind the aqueduct that his competitor was building. He gave up the race too. Only one man finished his aqueduct and brought fresh water to Caesarea. That was the man that the princess married.

If you walk around the town of Caesarea today you can see the ruins of two unfinished aqueducts that lead part of the way into town.

Which boyfriend do you think married the princess—the Muslim, the Jew, or the Christian? Nobody remembers. Maybe it's better that way.

Boys climb on the ruins of Caesarea's ancient aqueduct.
PHOTO COURTESY OF RIVKA MALAMUD.

Testament. Mohammed's neighbors laughed at him. "You're just repeating stories you heard from Christians and Jews in Mecca and Medina," they said.

After being sneered at, laughed at, and even threatened, Mohammed gathered some followers and ran away to the nearby town of Medina. There he taught more people about Allah and Islam. But the Jewish tribes of Mecca and Medina ignored him. Even though Mohammed turned toward Jerusalem to pray and observed the dietary laws of the Jews they would not accept him or his new religion. Mohammed was disappointed and insulted. "You Jews don't understand the true religion. The Jewish Bible is full of mistakes," he charged. He changed the rules to make Islam even more different from Judaism than it had been. He decided that Muslims must turn to Mecca instead of Jerusalem to pray. They would observe a day of prayer on Friday and fast all day during an entire month called Ramadan. But Muslims kept some Jewish laws. They circumcised their sons. They kept kosher. They stressed giving *tzedakah*, charity. And they accepted the holiness of leaders in the Bible like Abraham, Isaac, Ishmael, Jacob, and others. They also accepted the Hebrew prophets and Jesus as true prophets sent by God. "But our prophet Mohammed is the last of the prophets," said the Muslims, "after him there will be no more prophets."

Mohammed's followers wrote his desert vision and his later teachings in the Koran, the holy book of all Muslims. Then the Muslims turned to the other tribes of Arabia and persuaded them to become Muslims. If they couldn't be persuaded they faced the sharp swords of the true believers. Shouting, "*Allahu akbar!* (God is great)" the Muslims galloped out of the Arabian desert and carried the religion of Islam through the whole Middle East, North Africa, and into Europe. Today the lands on Israel's borders have mostly Muslim populations. And one-fifth of the world's population is Muslim.

Getting Back to the Yeast

Let's get back to baking hallah for a minute. You know that bubbling yeast concoctions can end up as pumpernickel bread, hallah, cinnamon raisin bread, or even coffee cake. They all look and taste different from each other. In the same way, when the Torah was mixed with the cultures of other peoples the result was two new religions that are very different from each other and very, very different from their original batter of Torah Judaism.

Calendar Counts

✦ The Jewish calendar starts with the biblical date for the creation of the world. The date comes 3,760 years before the general or Christian calendar begins. That makes the first year of the Jewish calendar about 5,760 years ago. For the exact year of today's Jewish calendar add 3,760 and the number of the general calendar year together.

✦ The Christian calendar begins with the date that Jesus was born. His birthday is year one. The general calendar used in the western world starts with this date too.

✦ The Muslim calendar starts with the year that Mohammed escaped from Mecca to the friendly town of Medina. That was in the year 622 of the general calendar. Subtract 622 from the general calendar year to find the Muslim year.

✦ So . . . if the general year and Christian year are 1999:

✦ The Jewish year is 5759, written in Hebrew as ה"תשנ"ט

✦ The Muslim year is 1377

A Brain Teaser

The Hebrew calendar shows the date in Hebrew letters. Each letter has a numerical value. Here's a chart of the numerical values ➡

70 —	ע	21—כא	11—יא	1 —	א
80 —	פ	22—כב	12—יב	2 —	ב
90 —	צ	23 — כג	13 — יג	3 —	ג
100 —	ק	24—כד	14—יד	4 —	ד
200 —	ר	25—כה	15—טו	5 —	ה
300 —	ש	26 — כו	16—טז	6 —	ו
400 —	ת	30 — ל	17 — יז	7 —	ז
500 —	תק	40 — מ	18—יח	8 —	ח
900—תתק		50 — נ	19—יט	9 —	ט
5000 — ה"		60 — ס	20 — כ	10 —	י

Great-Uncle Louie

If your Great-Uncle Louie died in ה"תרצ"ח, use the chart to figure out the date in numbers. That gives you the Jewish year. Now subtract 3760 from the Jewish year to get the general year.

Great-Uncle Louie passed away in 1938.

10 Coming Home to Israel

Great, Great, Great-Grandparents

People who live in Israel today find evidence of the Bible all around them. When Israeli kids go on hikes they may pick up bits of pottery made in the days of the Bible. When farmers plow their fields they often turn up building blocks or carved stones from ancient cities. And when builders dig the foundations for a new house they may uncover the walls of another house built during the time of the Bible. It's a little spooky until you remember that these finds are family heirlooms. The Jews of the old, biblical Land of Israel are the great, great, great-grandparents of modern Jews.

Of course people can forget their great, great-grandparents. They look at a faded picture in a photo album and ask, "Who's that?" And nobody knows the answer. But the Jewish people didn't forget about their ancestors and about the Land of Israel. They remembered their connection for 2,000 years until finally some Jews returned to their ancient land. They were like migrating birds who travel thousands of miles and still know exactly how to get back home. They have a homing instinct.

The Jewish homing instinct grew from the Torah with its laws and history and its reminders of the Land of Israel. Every century after the Jews left their land a few Jews would find their way back to Palestine. The great scholar Maimonides tried to settle in Palestine in 1200 c.e. A group of rabbis walked across Europe to reach Palestine in the 1500s. In the 1800s many Jews came from Yemen to settle in the Holy Land. All through the centuries old Jews came to Palestine to die because they wanted to be buried in holy soil. Others waited for the Messiah to bring them back.

Who are they?

Pioneers in Palestine

When the parents of your grandparents were alive, more than 100 years ago, some young Jews in Russia decided that they couldn't wait for the messiah any longer. They scraped together all their money and started out for the Holy Land. When the young people arrived they bought land from the Turkish or Arab owners, built their homes, and planted crops. We'll be the pioneers, they thought. Other Jews will leave Europe and join us . . . just as the Jews left Egypt and came to the Promised Land with

The children of Kfar Tabor stand in front of their small houses in 1913 with bare Mount Tabor looming behind them. They are all dressed up and seem to be waiting anxiously— for what? A wagonload of good things from the port of Jaffa? A famous visitor from Europe? A troop of much-feared Turkish soliders? We can only guess. PHOTO COURTESY OF WORLD ZIONIST ARCHIVES

Moses. The young pioneers were half right. Millions of Jews left Europe in the late 1800s and early 1900s. But they didn't go east to Palestine. They went in the opposite direction—to the United States.

Still a few stubborn, hopeful Jews kept coming to Palestine. They didn't find a land of milk and honey. Palestine was poor, rocky, and bare. The trees had been chewed up by goats or chopped down to build railroads. The streams and lakes were steamy swamps teeming with mosquitos. Small villages of Arab shepherds or farmers were scattered through the land. Sometimes neighboring Arabs stole cows or tools from the newcomers. Sometimes the Jewish settlers were attacked and killed in the fields. Their homing instincts had brought them to a hard, danger-ous place.

"Remember the Bible story about the Jews who returned from Babylonia?" they reminded each other. "They found a harsh land filled with enemies, just like we did. And they rebuilt the Temple holding a sword in one hand and a hammer in the other. If they could do it—we can do it!" Their parents wrote letters from Russia and Poland saying, "Darling, come home. Why should you suffer? When the Messiah comes he'll bring us all to the Holy Land." The young people wrote back to say, *"We'll* bring the Messiah!"

The pioneers stopped speaking the languages they knew best— Yiddish and Russian. Instead they struggled and stuttered and spoke only Hebrew, the language of the Bible. They thought up new Hebrew words for ice cream, cauliflower, bombs, and other modern objects to bring the language of the ancient prophets and kings into the nineteenth and twentieth centuries.

Meanwhile Jews and non-Jews outside Palestine were beginning to support the idea of Zionism, of building a country for the Jewish people. After the First World War when the Turkish rulers of Palestine were defeated the League of Nations (an early United Nations) gave the British the job of helping the Jews build a homeland in Palestine. Over the next twenty years the hills and fields turned green with forests and farms. Palestine began to bustle with new towns and factories as Jews and

Arabs from Europe and the Middle East streamed into the country.

World War II broke out in 1939. In the worst horror of that terrible war the German Nazis murdered most of the Jews of Europe, one third of all the Jews in the world. It was the most brutal destruction that Jews had ever known.

After the war Jewish survivors, Palestinian Jews, and people all over the world demanded that Great Britain keep its promise to set up a Jewish homeland in Palestine.

"No!" said the British. "There's no room for more Jews!"

SO THAT'S WHERE IT COMES FROM

So That's Where It Comes From!
Zionism

Zionism is the belief that the Land of Israel with its capital, Jerusalem, is the Jewish homeland. It all started with the Torah where God promised again and again to give this green land to God's people. Here are a few of the verses:

> The land into which you go is a land of hills and valleys, and drinks water of the rain of heaven. A land which the Lord, your God, cares for and watches over from the beginning of the year until the end.
>
> —DEUTERONOMY 11:11–12

> If you bring justice between man and his neighbor, if you do not oppress the stranger, the orphan and the widow . . . nor follow other gods . . . I will have you live in this land that I gave to your fathers forever and ever.
>
> —JEREMIAH 7:5–7

> Oh Jerusalem . . . there the [Hebrew] tribes used to go up . . . to give thanks to the Lord. There are the thrones of judgment, the thrones of the House of David. Pray for the peace of Jerusalem.
>
> —PSALMS 122:3–6

> I will bring back My people Israel. And they will rebuild the ruined cities and live in them. They will plant vineyards and drink their wine. They will make gardens and eat of their fruit. I will plant them on their land and they will not again be taken out of the land which I have given them, says the Lord your God.
>
> —AMOS 9:14–15

"Never!" said many of the Arabs in and around Palestine. "This is an Arab land!"

Fighting for a Homeland

But in 1947 the United Nations agreed that a Jewish and an Arab state should be established in Palestine. The Jews exploded with joy. They danced in the streets, lit bonfires, sang, and cheered. And they named their new state Israel, after the name of the biblical Land of Israel. But the Arabs refused to accept the Jewish state. Only one day after the new state was born, in May 1948, Arab armies attacked across all its borders.

There have been four major wars between Israel and its Arab neighbors since 1948. Just as in Bible days, Israel's most dangerous neighbors are in the northeast and in the south. In Bible times, Assyria and Babylonia were in the north and Egypt was in the south. Today Syria and Iraq are in the north and Egypt in the south. Yet there is hope for peace. Israel has signed peace treaties with some of her neighbors. Peace talks are going on with the others. Maybe the old Bible enemies will become friends some day.

In the meantime Jews have come home to Israel from all over the world. The Jews of Yemen came on huge Skymaster jets. They weren't scared, though they had never seen a plane before. After all, the Bible promised that "they should mount up with wings like eagles." The Jews of Ethiopia remembered their biblical ancestors King Solomon and the Queen of Sheba and left their mountain villages to come to Israel. In countries all over the world Jews remembered the promises of the prophets and came back to Israel.

This young soldier came to fight in the army of Israel after surviving the death camps of the Holocaust. His camp identification number is tattooed on his arm. PHOTO COURTESY OF WORLD ZIONIST ARCHIVES

The Bible in Super-Modern Israel

Modern Israelis are as modern as Americans are. They honk their car horns and speed along the highways talking on cellular phones. Tractors plow their fields. Cranes swing steel into place for giant office buildings. Kids kick soccer balls in the park, ride paddle boats on Lake Kinneret,

During the years of Jewish wandering, the Land of Israel became a magical place in people's imaginations. They pictured it as a green, sunny, happy land and told wistful stories about it. Like this one:

A Story: The She-Goats of Shebrezin

—adapted from a story in *Folktales of Israel*

A poor, pious Jew, his wife and their two goats lived in the woods near the small village of Shebrezin. Each morning the wife would tether the goats in a nearby field. In the evening she would bring them home and milk them. Then she and her husband would make butter and cheese from the milk and sell it to earn a living.

One afternoon she went to the field, but the goats were gone. She had forgotten to tether them. The poor woman rushed home crying, "We've lost the goats! How will we earn a living?" Her husband smiled and said calmly, "Don't worry. Everything comes from heaven." That evening the goats came home by themselves. And to the woman's surprise they gave more milk than ever. The next day she didn't tether them. And again they came home in the evening heavy with creamy, delicious milk. This happened for six days. On the seventh day the Jew decided to follow his goats and see where they went. He followed them through the woods and reached the dark opening of a cave. The goats trotted in and the man went after them. As he went further stones began to pound around him. "Everything comes from heaven," he said and kept on going. Suddenly screaming devils with flaming tongues sprang at him from the walls. He pulled his coat closer and kept going. Then gold coins and diamonds began to shower down and cover the ground. The Jew looked neither to the right nor to the left nor down at the ground—he went after the goats.

and play computer games. It doesn't look like a biblical scene at all. But the Bible is there. It's part of everyone's life whether he or she is religious or not.

Everyone does homework, shops, and does business in Hebrew, the language of the Bible. On the Biblical holidays of Sukkot, Passover, and

text continued on page 107

Far ahead the man saw bright sunlight. He walked until he stepped out into a green field sparkling with flowers. A boy sat on the grass playing a flute for the two goats. "Shalom Aleikhem," said the boy. "Welcome to the Holy Land."

The man began to tremble with joy. "Aleikhem Shalom," he answered. He realized that he was standing in the Land of Israel. The man fell to the ground and kissed the holy earth and then he quickly wrote a message to the people of his town and to all the Jews in exile. "Follow these goats. They will lead you to our blessed Land of Israel. Don't be afraid of the devils and the flames. Trust in heaven." He wrapped the message in a fig leaf and tied it to the neck of one of the goats.

The goats came back to the woman in the evening, without her husband. "My poor husband is lost!" cried the woman. She was so upset that she didn't notice the message in the fig leaf. The next morning she tethered the goats so they wouldn't run off and get lost like her husband. Then she waited and waited. After many days she decided sadly that her husband must have been killed by robbers. "I can't stay alone in the woods," she said to herself. So she moved to the village.

In her tiny village house the woman had no room for the two goats. She sold them to the butcher who slaughtered them. And then, too late, the butcher discovered the message from the pious Jew. He ran with it to the rabbi. The rabbi read it and burst into tears. "Now we'll never find the passage to the Holy Land," he wept. "We can only wait for the messiah and the Day of Redemption."

Moving Up
Tel Aviv moves up, up, up! Here's a new hotel rising near the beach. In the center of town office buildings loom up. And on the outskirts new multi-story apartment houses stand among green parks. PHOTO COURTESY OF MORDY BURSTEIN

Israeli kids take hikes and bus trips to Bible sites all over the country. This father and son are standing at the Kotel, an ancient wall of the Temple Mount. The Kotel has been holy to Jews for thousands of years because the First and Second Temples of Israel once stood above, on the Mount. PHOTO COURTESY OF ED TOBEN

Shavuot many Jewish Israelis crowd into Jerusalem and pray at the Western Wall of the ancient Temple Mount. They build *sukkot* on their balconies and in their yards. And they sing at their seders, "We were slaves in the Land of Egypt," just as Jews do outside Israel. Some adventurous Israelis even pack boxes of matzah into their cars and drive down to the Sinai desert for their Passover seder.

The Bible winks at you wherever you turn. Mount Tabor, where Deborah fought the Canaanites, looms above the valley of Jezreel. After a rain the deep, muddy soil traps the tractor wheels just as it once trapped the wheels of Yavin's chariots. The sun bakes down on hikers in the Judean desert as fiercely as it did on Elijah the prophet when he was hiding from Queen Jezebel. Fishing boats take off from the port of Jaffa where the prophet Jonah once set sail to escape from God. And people still come to Mount Moriah and the Temple Mount to pray in the same place that Abraham prepared to sacrifice his son Isaac to God.

Great scenery . . . but that's only part of the story. Archaeologists find out more of the story by digging into the earth. They want to hold the past in their hands. They want to understand how the long-gone Israelis lived and maybe to prove that the Bible stories really happened.

Let's go digging in the next chapter.

The Port of Jaffa on a Quiet, Early Morning
Jaffa is now part of the modern city of Tel Aviv, but the docks smell as fishy as they did in the days of the prophet Jonah. Fishing boats, tourists, and restaurants keep the port busy.

Bible Quizzes

Modern Israel's first prime minister, David Ben-Gurion, was small and roly-poly with wispy, white hair and powerful determination. He led the young country while it fought for its life. His love for the Bible helped Ben-Gurion through very hard times. He wanted other Jews to study Bible too, so he started a yearly Bible quiz open to Jewish children all over the world. The quiz is still held in Jerusalem each year. The questions are tough! Try these:

1. What was the name of the King of Elam?

   the answer is in Genesis 14:9

2. Which peoples joined Shishak in his campaign against Jerusalem?

   the answer is in II Chronicles 12:3

3. What happens to a person who eats blood in any form?

   the answer is in Leviticus 7:27

You had to be a Bible Brain to answer those questions. See how you do on these easier ones. Ten correct answers make you a genius. Seven to nine, a scholar. Four to six, a sleepy scholar. One to three, uh-oh, better reread Chapters Two, Three, and Four!

1. Which did God create first, the sun and moon or the animals and birds?

   Answer: Sun and moon

2. Why did the angel give Abraham a ram to sacrifice?

   Answer: God sent the ram to be used as a sacrifice instead of Abraham's son, Isaac

3. Why did Pharaoh command that all Hebrew boy babies be drowned?

   Answer: Pharaoh was afraid that there were too many Hebrews in Egypt

4. How many plagues did God send down onto Pharaoh and his people?

   Answer: Ten

5. How many years did the Hebrew tribes wander in the desert after Egypt?

   Answer: Forty

6. Who became leader of the tribes after Moses died?

   Answer: Joshua

7. Which woman was a judge over the tribes?

   Answer: Deborah

8. Which prophet spent time inside a big fish?
Answer: Jonah

9. Who told King David the story about the rich man with big flocks of sheep and the poor man with only one, small lamb?
Answer: The prophet Nathan

10. Which great prophets said, "Nation shall not lift up sword against nation"?
Answer: Micah and Isaiah

SILLY BIBLE QUESTIONS °°°°°°VERY SILLY BIBLE QUESTIONS

Now if your brain needs to rest try these silly Bible questions:

1. **Why couldn't the animals play cards on Noah's ark?**
Answer: Because Noah sat on the deck.

2. **How did the Queen of Sheba's camel get to the top of an oak tree?**
Answer: He sat on an acorn and waited.

3. **How did the camel get down?**
Answer: He sat on a leaf and waited for fall.

4. **What baseball team did Goliath play on?**
Answer: The Giants, of course.

5. **How many family members came to eat in the *sukkah* that Moses built?**
Answer: Three sisters, two uncles, and 10,000 ants.

6. **When did Joseph play tennis?**
Answer: When he served in Pharaoh's court.

7. **If you were walking in the desert and saw Goliath waking up from his nap, what time would it be?**
Answer: Time to run.

8. **Who was the best actor in the Bible?**
Answer: Samson. He brought down the house.

11

Bible Detectives or Scientific Snoops?

You wouldn't go snooping in someone's kitchen, opening closets, peeking in the oven, and even sorting through the garbage. At the most you might take a quick look in the cookie jar. But archaeologists go snooping all the time. It's not called snooping when the owner of the kitchen has been dead for 2,000 years. It's called the science of archaeology. And the scientists, the archaeologists, are detectives of the past who search patiently for evidence of the ways people lived long, long ago.

A Giant Layer Cake

Where in Israel should an archaeologist start looking? Every place! Israel is like a giant layer cake. The icing on the top layer holds the farms and cities and roadways of modern Israel. When farmers dig down a few feet to plow a field or when builders dig foundations for a house, they reach another layer of the cake. They may begin to turn up bits of pottery, square-shaped stones, old tools, bones, and other things that come from an earlier time in history. Then the archaeologists race up in their jeeps, shoo away the farmers or builders, and begin to dig very carefully down through the layers of earth and rock.

Archaeologists examine every bit of pottery and every rock that has been cut and shaped. Just as you can tell the difference between a Model T Ford and a brand-new car, an archaeologist can tell the difference between the designs and colors on bits of pottery from different times and places. He or she can look at a carved, stone figure, a coffin, or a bit of jewelry and decide which people made it, and when.

Telling about Tells

It is easy to understand the layers of human settlement when we look at a tell, which is a rounded hill that isn't made of rock like ordinary hills. It's made of towns built on top of each other. People might have built the first town, the one at the bottom of the tell, beside a clear spring or stream. After many years enemies may have attacked the town, killed the people, or driven them away and smashed the houses. Prickly thistles and wild oats sprouted between the stones of the walls. Dust, earth, and leaves slowly covered the ruins, forming a low mound. After a while new

Diagram of a Tell

Telling about Sasa

The kibbutz, or "collective village," of Sasa in northern Israel is built on a tell, which is an ancient hill. Once it was on the midpoint of a road that led from Damascus, Syria, to the Mediterranean Sea. For at least 5,000 years people have been building their homes in this place, one on top of the other. PHOTO COURTESY OF MORDY BURSTEIN

Slicing the Tell

When we cut slices from the tell of Sasa we find remains of these earlier settlements.

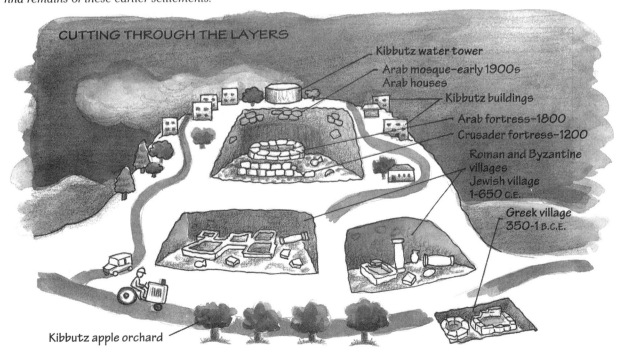

CUTTING THROUGH THE LAYERS

Kibbutz water tower
Arab mosque–early 1900s
Arab houses
Kibbutz buildings
Arab fortress–1800
Crusader fortress–1200
Roman and Byzantine villages
Jewish village 1–650 C.E.
Greek village 350–1 B.C.E.

Kibbutz apple orchard

people came. They liked the little stream and built their houses on the mound beside it. Years later the newcomers might have been driven off by enemies too, or disease may have killed them. The stream may have dried up during a long spell without rain. Then the people would have packed up and gone off to find new homes near water. Their leftover houses would form another layer. With each new settlement the tell grew higher.

Each layer of a tell has a sad or exciting story to tell. For instance, in a layer deep under the city of Jerusalem archaeologists uncovered a family kitchen from the time of the Second Temple, 2,000 years ago. Huge jars for grain, oil, and dried fruit stand by the walls. A clay oven is ready for a batch of pita bread. But the walls and jars are black from the soot of a great fire. Could it have been the fire that broke out when the Romans destroyed the Temple and the city in 70 C.E.? "Maybe," say the archaeologists. Then what happened to the family? We can only guess.

The Dead Sea Scrolls

Instead of digging into the earth archaeologists sometimes have to climb mountains. One day a Bedouin shepherd boy made an exciting discovery in a cave high on a cliff near the Dead Sea in a place called Qumran. He had climbed the cliff to hunt for a runaway goat. When he saw a dark cave opening he thought, aha that's where she hid. He tossed in a stone. But instead of a frightened "meh-eh-eh" he heard the sound of breaking pottery. The boy had discovered a treasure of huge, covered jars filled with scrolls. Jews had carried the scrolls up to the cave almost 2,000 years earlier to protect them from their Roman enemies. Archaeologists carefully unrolled the stiff, dry leather of the scrolls. One of the scrolls was made of thin copper which was stuck together and almost impossible to unroll. They had found the oldest written text of the Bible ever discovered—almost all of the writings of the prophet Isaiah, written in clear Hebrew letters that can easily be read today, as well as documents written in ancient Hebrew script. There are also sections from other prophets and writings of a group of Jews called Essenes. They tell us about the ideas swirling around in those years of Roman oppression and Jewish rebellion.

Just getting his hands on the scrolls was a dangerous adventure for a brave Israeli archaeologist. The Bedouin boy found the scrolls soon before Israel's War of Independence in 1948. At that time the city of

Good Insurance?

Little figures of women like these are found in digs all over Israel. They aren't dolls. They're goddesses. In spite of the prophets' angry warnings against worshipping false gods, many Israelis continued to keep the small household gods. They prayed to the Lord and they also prayed to the idols. An idol in the hand as well as God in the heavens must have seemed like good insurance to them. When Rebecca had to leave her home and go off to marry Isaac she brought along a small idol to help keep her safe. This clay figure was made about 2600 years ago and found at Lachish in Israel.

Jerusalem was divided into two warring halves. The Bedouin gave a few bits of scroll to a merchant in the Arab part of Jerusalem. The merchant called his friend Eliezer Sukenik, a well known Israeli archaeologist. Sukenik hurried to the barbed wire fence that divided the city. He examined the pieces through the fence and shivered with excitement. They were the oldest pieces of parchment he had ever seen and the Hebrew writing was clear and perfect. What a wonderful gift for the new State of Israel. He had to buy them! Sukenik made secret, dangerous trips into enemy territory to negotiate for and finally to buy the precious scrolls. In the end everyone was happy. The Bedouin boy got his money, the merchant got paid, the Israelis got their ancestors' wonderful, ancient scrolls . . . but the goat . . . whatever happened to the runaway goat?

A Grim Bible Battle

Northeast of Israel, in Iraq, archaeologists dug the great city of Nineveh out of an earthen tell. This is the city that the rebellious prophet Jonah was sent to save. The diggers uncovered large palaces guarded by winged bulls with human heads. The most exciting finds for Bible scholars were thirteen stone slabs covered with carved pictures and writings. They show the Assyrian king, Sennacherib, sitting on a hill watching as his army conquered and looted a city. The writing tells that Sennacherib was watching booty being carried from the Judean city of Lachish.

Many years later archaeologists found the buried city of Lachish in southern Israel. It was the same city that Sennacherib had captured. As they dug they found hundreds of Assyrian arrow heads. And when they uncovered the city walls they found that they looked just like the carved pictures on Sennacherib's stone slabs.

text continued on page 116

The Conquest of Lachish

Fighting Wars in Bible Days

This drawing based on King Sennacherib's stone slabs shows exactly how people fought wars during Bible times. They were as bloody as modern wars, but axes and boiling oil don't hit as many people as bombs do, so fewer people got hurt.

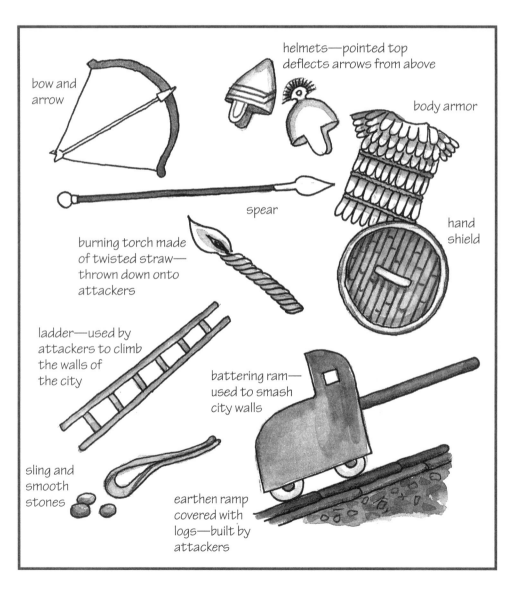

bow and arrow

helmets—pointed top deflects arrows from above

body armor

spear

burning torch made of twisted straw—thrown down onto attackers

hand shield

ladder—used by attackers to climb the walls of the city

battering ram—used to smash city walls

sling and smooth stones

earthen ramp covered with logs—built by attackers

Bible Times Warrior
This archer is taking aim from behind a tall, standing shield.

Victory Stele
*The letters carved into this stone in
the Aramaic alphabet tell of a victory
by the King of Aram over the "House
of David."* PHOTO BY ZEV RADOVAN,
COURTESY OF NELSON GLUECK SCHOOL OF
BIBLICAL ARCHAEOLOGY

Proving the Bible

Was there really a Moses or a Deborah or a King David? For some people the words of the Bible are good enough. They don't need proof. But bit by bit archaeologists are finding physical proof of some of the Bible stories. Both the "show-me" people and the "I believe every word" people are pleased. At a dig in Tel Dan in Northern Israel archaeologists dug carved stones out of the wall of an ancient building. They were part of a stone sign post put up by one of the kings of Aram—today it's Syria—about 3,000 years ago. The carved letters boast of a great victory over Israel and the House of David. Archaeologists would've kissed the boastful, old King of Aram if they could have. He gave them the proof, carved in stone, that David and his kingdom really existed!

Hezekiah's Tunnel

King Hezekiah of Judah left solid evidence of his reign. In the Second Book of Kings the Bible tells us that he had a tunnel dug from a spring outside the wall of Jerusalem. The water from the spring flowed through the tunnel, under the wall, to a pool inside the city. Even if enemies surrounded the wall of the city its people would always have water to drink.

On a hot, summer day one hundred years ago a schoolboy found proof of the Bible story. He went wading in an old tunnel under Jerusalem to cool off. Suddenly he slipped and fell. When he grabbed at the wall to get up he touched a strangely smooth stone with letters carved into the surface. The boy told his friends about the stone. Soon an archaeologist heard the story. He crept into the tunnel, copied the writing by candlelight and made a cast of the stone's face. The writing was found to be ancient Hebrew script that had been used at the time of Hezekiah. It told how two teams of men had started chopping a tunnel through solid rock. One team was inside the city. One was outside. They cut toward each other until they finally met in the middle. And there they set the smooth stone to tell of their hard work.

The smooth stone has disappeared. Someone pried it from the tunnel wall. But you can still explore Hezekiah's 2,500-year-old tunnel when you come to Israel. Hezekiah forgot the light bulbs so be sure to bring a candle.

Archaeology Goes to War

In modern times archaeologists and soldiers worked together to win an important battle. It happened during Israel's War of Independence. The enemy Egyptians were encamped across the only road leading south through the Israeli desert to the Egyptian border. Deep desert sand surrounded the road. Only vehicles with tracks like tanks could go through the sand to bypass the Egyptians. But in those days Israel had no tanks. They only had trucks. The trucks would have to follow the road and then the waiting Egyptians would blast them to pieces. Luckily the Israeli army's chief of operations was also an expert archaeologist. He remembered that a 2,000-year-old Roman road had once stretched across this part of the desert. Scouts went out and found the road, hidden by sand. Quickly the trucks were loaded with Israeli soldiers. They bounced along the ancient stone road, circled the Egyptians, and chased them back across the border.

Adventurers, Crazies, and Treasure Hunters

There are still a million questions to answer and mysteries to solve about the Bible.

Where is Noah's ark?

Where are the gold, silver, and precious stones of the Second Temple?

What happened to the Ten Commandments and the Ark of the Covenant?

Every few years adventurers form an expedition to climb to the snow-covered top of Mount Ararat in Turkey. They believe that Noah's ark landed there and is waiting to be found. And treasure hunters still search the caves and rocks of the Judean Desert. They're sure that the priests of the Second Temple hid the Temple's treasures in the desert before the Romans could steal them. Some people are convinced that the Ark of the Covenant was taken from the Holy of Holies in the First Temple and carried to Ethiopia. They say that today the Ark is hidden behind the barred doors of an ancient church in Axum. But no outsider is allowed into the church to check the story.

Though treasure hunters are still searching for the Bible's lost, ancient treasures, the Bible's teachings have never been lost. In the next chapter let's look at Bible customs in our daily lives.

How Old Are You, Mummy?

Until fifty years ago archaeologists had to guess at the age of ancient bits of cloth or bone. Then they worked out a system called carbon dating. No more guesswork! Here's how it works:

Anything that's alive contains carbon. You, me, plants, and animals all contain carbon. When the creature or plant dies the carbon begins to leave at a slow, regular rate. Archaeologists measure how much carbon is left in each dead creature or plant that they are investigating. Then they can figure out how many years have passed since the thing was alive.

12

The Bible and You

You've reached the last chapter! Now you know a little about archaeology, a little about life in the days of the Bible, and a little about the importance of the Bible in Jewish history. But how about you, yourself, today? Do you know about your own connections to the Bible? You'll find some of them in this chapter.

Bible Customs in Jewish Life

Pidyon ha-ben
Four generations meet to celebrate the birth of a baby boy. The parents pay a silver dollar to the Kohen standing to the right of the baby to symbolically free him from service in the Temple. PHOTO COURTESY OF JULIE BURSTEIN

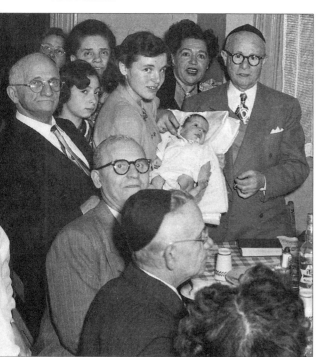

If you're a boy you were probably circumcised when you were eight days old. Why? Because the Bible tells that circumcision is a sign of God's agreement or covenant with the Jewish people. Abraham, the first Jew, circumcised his sons Ishmael and Isaac. If you're a girl, your name was probably read aloud during the reading of the Torah in the synagogue after you were born.

When you turn twelve or thirteen you may become a bat or bar mitzvah. Why? Because the Mishnah, a book that grew from the Bible, says that at age thirteen a boy is responsible for his own actions. A girl is responsible at age twelve! At your Bar Mitzvah and at many Bat Mitzvahs, you'll be called up to the reading of the Torah scroll in the synagogue and you will read the haftorah, a part of the Book of Prophets. Then everyone will throw candy at you. That's an extra. There's no rule about throwing candy in the Bible.

At religious school you study Hebrew, the language of the Torah. Why? So that you will be able to read the Torah and the Hebrew prayers in the prayer book, as Jews have done since Bible days. And you stand facing Jerusalem when you pray because that's where the Holy Temple once stood.

You might get off from school on the Jewish holidays that are called holy days in the Bible: Sukkot, Passover, Shavuot, and of course Shabbat (Saturday).

When you get married, if you are the bridegroom, you may stomp on a glass and break it. Why? To remember the destruction of the lost, Holy Temple in Jerusalem. And some day you may visit Israel to see the Land of the Bible, now

These objects are used to follow Bible commandments during holidays and in daily life.

Torah scroll

shofar

tefillin

menorah

sukkah

tallit (prayer shawl)

matzah (unleavened bread)

Shabbat candlesticks

lulav and etrog

kiddush cup

mezuzzah

rebuilt into a modern country. Next to the new buildings in Jerusalem you'll find the Kotel, a wall of the ancient Temple Mount of Bible days, still standing. Like many Jews over the last twenty centuries you may write a note to God and stick it between the great stones of the Wall.

Bible Names

The Bible is a great source of Hebrew names. Parents-to-be search the Bible or books of names that are based on the Bible to find the perfect name. Sometimes they don't have to search because there's a name already waiting. If the family is Ashkenazi, originally from most of eastern and western Europe, the new baby may be given the name of a family member who has died. If the family is Sephardi, originally from most of southern Europe, Asia, and North Africa, the baby may be named after a living relative. So the new baby's name will help the family to honor and remember the person who carried it first. If you are Leah, Daniel, Judith, Joseph, Sarah, or Joshua, you have a tie to your Bible namesake and to the grandparent or other relative after whom you are named.

Jews use their Hebrew names at all important turning points of their lives. When you are born, become bar and bat mitzvahed, married, perhaps get divorced, and when you die, your Hebrew name will be used. In the synagogue people are called up to read the Torah by their Hebrew first names, followed by the Hebrew first names of their parents. For example, if your name is David, your father is Michael and your mother is Miriam, the rabbi or the *shammash*, "rabbinic asssistant", of a liberal synagogue will call out: "Let David, son of Michael and Miriam come up." A traditional rabbi or *shammash* will use your name and your father's name.

Here's a list of some Bible names. You've read about many of these people in the earlier chapters.

Girl's Name	Bible Person with That Name	Nickname or Related Name
Abigail	one of the wives of King David	Abby, Gail
Abra	girl's name for Abraham, the first Jew	
Ada	wife of Lamech, a descendant of Cain	Addie, Adi
Bathsheba	wife of King David, Solomon's mother	
Beth	House of God	
Carmela	Mount Carmel where Elijah met the priests of Baal	
Dana	girl's name for Dan, one of the 12 Hebrew tribes	
Danielle	girl's name for Daniel, who slept in a lion's den	
Davida	girl's name for David, King of Israel	
Delilah	Samson's lover and betrayer	Lila
Deborah	judge and prophetess who fought the Canaanites	Debbie
Dina	daughter of Jacob and Leah	
Eden	the very first garden, the Garden of Eden	Edna
Eliya	girl's name for Elijah	
Elizabeth	wife of Moses' brother Aaron	Liz, Eliza, Lisa, Beth, Elisheva

A rabbi ordered a pair of pants from a tailor. "I'll bring them to you within a week," said the tailor. The week passed—no pants. Finally, the tailor arrived three days late. The rabbi tried on the pants. They were perfect. "They're fine," he said as he paid the tailor, "but explain to me why you were late. The Lord took six days to create the whole world and it took you ten days to make one pair of pants."

"Just look at my work," said the tailor, "it's perfect. Now look at God's world."

		Nickname or Related Name
Esther	heroine of Purim, wife of King Ahasuerus	**Esti**
Eve	the first woman, wife of Adam	**Evelyn, Eva**
Gabrielle	girl's name for the angel Gabriel	**Gabi, Gabriela**
Hannah	mother of Samuel the high priest and prophet	**Anne, Anna**
Jessica	a relative of Abraham	**Jess, Jessie**
Judith	girl's name for Judah, one of the twelve tribes; also a heroine in a later book added to the Bible	**Judy**
Leah	Jacob's wife and Rachel's sister	**Lee**
Meirav	King Saul's older daughter	
Michal	King Saul's younger daughter	**Michelle, Mickey**
Miriam	sister of Moses and Aaron, and Moses' babysitter	**Mimi, Miri**
Naomi	Ruth's Israelite mother-in-law	
Penina	wife of Elkanah who was Samuel's father	**Penny**
Rachel	Leah's sister, Jacob's wife	**Rae, Rochelle**
Rebecca	Isaac's wife, mother of Jacob and Esau	**Becky, Rivka**
Ruth	Naomi's Moabite daughter-in-law, King David's great-grandmother	
Sarah	matriarch of the Jewish people, Abraham's wife	
Sharon	the coastline of Israel	**Shari**
Shulamit	woman in the love poems of King Solomon	**Shula**
Tamar	King David's daughter	**Tammy**
Yael	killer of the Canaanite general Sisera	**Yoli**
Yona	a dove (Noah sent a dove to check the waters)	**Yonat**

Boy's Name	*Bible Person with That Name*	*Nickname or Related Name*
Aaron	Moses' older brother and his spokesman	
Abel	Cain's brother, the first murder victim	
Abner	general of King Saul's army	
Abraham	patriarch of the Jewish people, made a covenant with God, Sarah's husband	**Avi, Abe, Bram**
Adam	the first man, Eve's husband	
Amos	a fiery prophet	
Arieh	a lion, a symbol used in the ark	**Ari**
Asher	Jacob's son, one of the twelve tribes	
Baruch	loyal friend and helper of Jeremiah the prophet	
Benjamin	Jacob's beloved youngest son, one of the twelve tribes	**Ben, Benjie**

NICE KITTIES

Dan	Jacob's son, one of the twelve tribes	**Danny**
Daniel	Babylonian Jew who was thrown into a den of hungry lions	**Danny**
David	second King of Israel	**Dave, Duddy**
Eli	blind high priest who was Samuel's teacher	
Elijah	prophet who defeated the priests of Baal	**Eli**
Elisha	prophet and follower of Elijah	
Ezekiel	prophet during the exile in Babylonia	**Zeke**
Gabriel	angel who saved Daniel from the lions	**Gabe, Gabi**
Gideon	judge over the tribes and soldier	**Gidi**
Hiram	King of Tyre, King Solomon's friend	**Hy**
Isaac	son of Abraham and Sarah	
Israel	Jacob's name and the name of the Jewish people	**Izzy**
Jacob	son of Isaac and Rebecca	**Jake**
Jeremiah	prophet and leader before the exile to Babylonia	**Jerry**
Joel	prophet	
Jonah	the prophet that was swallowed by a big fish	
Jonathan	King Saul's son and David's best friend	**Jon**
Joseph	son of Jacob and Rachel who became a prince in Egypt	**Joe**
Joshua	led the Hebrew tribes into the Promised Land	**Josh**
Judah	one of the twelve tribes, name of the smaller kingdom after Israel split in two	
Levi	tribe of priests who took care of the ark and the Temple	
Micah	a prophet	**Mickey**
Michael	an angel	**Mike**
Moses	prophet, teacher, and leader who brought the Jews out of Egypt, brother of Miriam and Aaron	**Moe**
Nathan	prophet who scolded King David	**Nate, Nat**
Noah	built the ark and rode out the flood with pairs of all living things	
Reuben	Jacob's son, one of the twelve tribes	
Samson	judge over the tribes and the strongest man in Israel	**Sam**
Samuel	young priest's helper who became a prophet and high priest	**Sam**
Saul	first king of Israel	
Seth	son of Adam and Eve, Cain's younger brother	
Simon	Jacob's son, one of the twelve tribes	
Solomon	wise king who built the Temple in Jerusalem	**Sol**
Uriah	Bathsheba's first husband, officer in David's army	**Uri**

The Bible in Movies, Music, and Art

Black slaves loved Bible stories and they told the stories in songs called "spirituals." The spiritual "Go Down Moses" tells how God ordered Moses to go down to Egypt and make Pharaoh free the Jews. Today many families sing it at their Passover seder. Another spiritual tells how Joshua "fit the battle of Jericho and the walls came tumbling down." The slaves sang their spirituals and forgot their hard lives for a short while.

Operas like *Samson and Delilah* and musical works like Handel's *Messiah* and Leonard Bernstein's *Jeremiah* are based on the Bible. Plays and movies tell Bible stories too. For instance the *Raiders of the Lost Ark* is an exciting, adventure-filled movie that tracks Moses' Holy Ark through dens of poisonous snakes, over wild mountains and into the depths of the Pentagon's cellars. *Joseph and the Amazing Technicolor Dreamcoat* is a funny musical play about Jacob's dreamy son who was sold as a slave and ended up a prince of Egypt.

Artists all over the world have painted and sculpted people and scenes from the Bible. Rembrandt, Michelangelo, Chagall, and many more artists have made great figures like Moses, David, and Ruth come alive for us.

Bible Place Names

Religious pilgrims were among the earliest European settlers of North America. The Old and New Testaments were often the only books in their homes. And they read the "Good Book" whenever they could find time. Names of heroes and heroines of the Bible became favorite names for their children. The place names of the Bible were used for towns, mountains, and rivers all over the United States and Canada. There's a town of Palestine in Texas and a Mount Nebo (named after the mountain Moses climbed before he died) in Utah. Jericho (whose walls fell down before Joshua and the Hebrews) is a town in New York. Promised Land is in Arkansas and Beersheba in Tennessee.

The people of Italy sent this statue of young King David, sculpted by the Italian fifteenth-century artist Verrocchio, to the city of Jerusalem as a gift for the city's three-thousandth birthday.

text continued on page 125

So That's Where It Comes From!
Everyday Bible Phrases

Bible's Words	How They Are Used in the Bible	How They Are Used Today
Am I my brother's keeper? —TORAH, GENESIS 4:9–10	After Cain killed Abel, God asked Cain where his brother was. This was his answer.	I'm not going to worry about someone else, so don't blame me for something he or she did.
A man after his own heart. —PROPHETS, SAMUEL 13:14	God was looking for a king to rule over Israel who would follow God's laws.	A person we like, who thinks like we do.
A scapegoat —TORAH, LEVITICUS 16:10	A goat who was sent away into the desert on Yom Kippur, carrying the sins of the people.	Someone who gets picked on or blamed for everything.
Spare the rod and spoil the child. —WRITINGS, PROVERBS 13:24	A proverb that gives advice on raising children—you may not agree.	Teach children by spanking them whenever necessary.
There's nothing new under the sun. —WRITINGS, ECCLESIASTES 1:9	Some believe these are the words of King Solomon as a sad, tired old man.	Everything has already been tried or done. There aren't any new ideas.
Eat, drink, and be merry. —WRITINGS, ECCLESIASTES 8:15	King Solomon or Kohelet said, "Enjoy yourselves. This is the best thing to do in life."	Have fun!
The leopard cannot change his spots. —PROPHETS, JEREMIAH 13:23	Jeremiah scolded the people and said they would never learn to do right.	People can't change the way they behave.
(It's just) a drop in the bucket. —PROPHETS, ISAIAH 40:15	The peoples of the world are very small compared to the greatness of God.	When a great deal of work or money or thinking is needed to do a big job, but only a little is found.
Out of the mouths of babes. —WRITINGS, PSALMS 8:1–2	Praise of God can come even from the very young.	Even the simplest, youngest person can say wise things.
The apple of his eye. —TORAH, DEUTERONOMY 32:10	God is describing God's love for Israel which is protected as carefully as the pupil of God's eye.	Your favorite person.

A Bible Pun
When Abraham decided to upgrade his PC to Windows 99, Isaac couldn't believe it. "Dad," he said, "your old PC doesn't have enough memory." Abraham answered, "My son, God will provide the RAM."

Here are the most popular names for towns:

Salem (from *shalom*, meaning "peace") comes first with 32 namesakes. Next comes Lebanon (home of the cedar trees that King Solomon used to build the Temple) with 22 namesakes. Runners-up are Bethel, Hebron, Canaan, and Shilo. They are all names of places in the Bible.

The state of Utah has many sites named after Bible places because the Mormons who settled there were serious Bible readers. For instance, Utah's Jordan River runs into the Great Salt Sea just as the biblical Jordan River runs into the salty Dead Sea of Israel. Also in Utah there's a huge park full of steep, colorful cliffs that's called Zion National Park.

When you go on a trip watch the signposts. See how many Bible names you can find.

Two Fun Ideas

Grandparents, parents, and kids in a Michigan congregation dressed up in sheets and bathrobes. Then they followed a trail of paper footprints from the classrooms to the social hall. At the door, teachers snapped Polaroid photos of each person and glued the photos into passports for the journey to the land of the Bible.

An enormous tent with a straw-covered floor filled the side of the social hall. On pillows in one corner sat a make-believe Abraham and Sarah. They stamped the passports and told the story of God's promise to Abraham and of the long, dangerous journey that Abraham, Sarah, and their family took over mountains and deserts to reach the Land of Israel. In another corner the brothers Jacob and Esau acted out an angry, screaming argument about birthrights. At the end they asked the guests to judge between them. Jacob's son, Joseph, sat in a third corner and taught the grown-ups how to say a blessing over their children.

The next stop was in the gym for a Bible feast. A long table waited, piled

Bibles are found in nine out of ten American homes. Can you find yours? Bibles often become family histories as people write on the flyleaf the names and dates when family members are born, marry, and die.

high with pita bread, olives, cheeses, dates, figs, and jugs of wine and grape juice.

Finally, at the front door the passports were stamped again. The guests took off their sheets and bathrobes, waved goodbye to Bible country, and came back to the twentieth (almost twenty-first) century.

Kite makers in California designed a twirling, barrel-shaped kite with help from the biblical prophet, Zechariah. In the book of Zechariah 5:2, the prophet describes a flying scroll twenty cubits long and ten cubits wide. "If ten by twenty worked for Zechariah, we'll try it too," said the kite makers.

High above California's beaches, the kite flies and spins. It turns opposite to the wind's direction, fighting the current just as the prophets always did.

Summing Up: A Different Olympic Race

Jews are the longest distance runners in the world. They'd surely win the Olympic Competition for National Survival—if there were such a race. Over the centuries people of many lands and religions were driven from their homes. They disappeared into their new lands like raindrops into the ocean. Some Jewish communities disappeared too, like the Jews of Kaifeng, China. But many others held on to their faith in God and their feeling of being part of the Jewish people wherever they lived.

Why?

Because of the Torah.

The Torah gave Jews special gifts which held them together. Some of these gifts are: a belief in one God, religious laws, holidays and customs, the Hebrew language, a shared homeland in the Land of Israel, and moral guidance for their daily lives.

It's more than 2,000 years since the Torah was written in the form we know it today. Life has changed. Most of us aren't farmers or shepherds anymore. We don't ride camels and donkeys (except at the zoo), or eat balls of goat cheese for breakfast. The culture around us often teaches us to care about things that the Torah doesn't value. It tells us to make a lot of money, buy a big house and expensive clothing, worry about our appearance (prettier is better), and think of ourselves—number one—before others.

Once, prophets were sent by God to stand at the Temple gate and teach the Torah's law. But today there aren't any prophets in the shopping centers or the town square. Each of us has to juggle the modern values and the Torah values in his or her own life. And we have to think of the Torah's gifts and how to use them. Here are a few ways. See if you can think of more:

✦ Look around at the green, beautiful world and thank God for it and take care of it.
✦ Respect and care about your parents, brothers and sisters, and other people. Treat them the same way you'd like them to treat you.
✦ Celebrate and enjoy Shabbat and other Jewish holidays.

It's tricky to juggle Torah values and modern values. But Jews are good at it. They've been juggling for more than 2,200 years. So watch your step, Bible reader, and keep juggling and keep running in this record-breaking Olympic marathon.

Isaiah the prophet lived in a time of war and fear of war, just as many people do today. But he promised that peace would come to the world one day. His words are inscribed on the Isaiah Wall at the United Nations in New York. PHOTO COURTESY OF MORDY BURSTEIN

Bible Crafts: Dress up the Torah

In Italy, Jewish women took their fine silk wedding dresses, brightly colored and embroidered with gold thread, the prettiest dresses they would ever own, and cut them up to make curtains for the ark, the closet that holds the Torah. In central Europe mothers took the long cloths that had been wrapped around their newborn babies, embroidered them with words from the Torah and the name of the child, and brought them to the synagogue to be used to wrap around the Torah scrolls. And in modern Israel when second graders start studying Torah their parents make a beautiful cloth cover for their Torah textbook. They paint or embroider the child's name and a special design on the cloth. Nobody makes beautiful, handmade covers for math, science, or language study textbooks. Torah study is special.

Here is how to make a cover for your favorite book of Bible stories. You can cover any other favorite book the same way.

You will need:

2 pieces of stiff cardboard, each piece 1/8 inch wider on all sides than your book
white glue
a ruler
for spine, a strip of cloth, about 2 inches wide and 3 inches longer than the height of the book
for cover, 2 pieces of cloth or paper, 2 inches wider than the cardboard on top, bottom, and outside edges
ribbon, at least 12 inches long
for end papers, 2 sheets of colored paper, 1/4 inch smaller on all sides than each piece of cardboard
for decorating the cover, colored marking pens, glitter, paint, felt, etc.

Follow these steps:

1. Glue the two pieces of cardboard onto the cloth strip. The cloth strip will be the spine. Leave a space down the center as wide as the thickness of your book. The extra cloth will be at the top and bottom.
2. Fold the extra cloth over onto the inside of the cardboard and glue.
3. Glue two pieces of ribbon to the outside of the cardboard as shown.

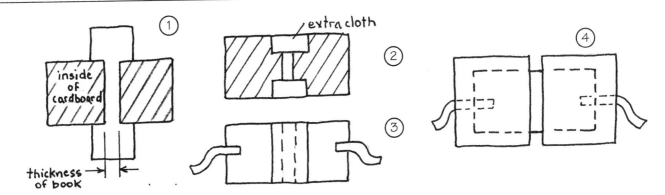

4. Glue the two pieces of the cover cloth or paper to the outside of the cardboard. The extra paper or cloth should be at the top, bottom and outer side.

5. Trim the corners of the cover cloth or paper as shown. With an X-acto knife or small scissors cut a slit as wide as the ribbon on the edge of the cover cloth. Thread the ribbon through the slit so that it hangs on the outside of the cover.

6. Fold the cover cloth or paper onto the inside of the cardboard and glue.

7. Glue the two end papers onto the inside of the cardboard and over the folded-over cover paper.

8. Let the glue dry for at least 3 hours. Decorate the cover with the book's title and Bible story designs or other designs. Draw directly on the cover or cut out shapes and paste them on. Rainbows, Noah's ark, Ten Commandments, flowers, lightning, the sun and moon . . . you choose.

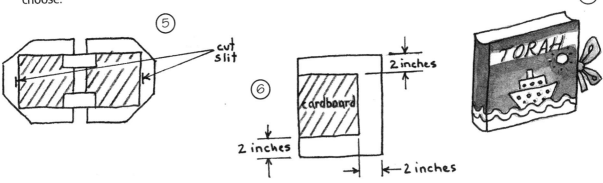

13

The End
(or the Beginning)

When the Messiah Comes

In the middle of your social studies homework you hear a loud, humming sound coming from the backyard. Bright lights flash through the kitchen window.

"STEV?" you wonder aloud. "It's the STEV!" you realize. "Get off the tomato plants!" you scream and race out the back door. The STEV is floating two inches above the vegetable patch with its door wide open. You jump into the cabin and slam the door. The STEV begins to rise.

"Wel-come-a-board," creaks the familiar voice (if it's not familiar please reread Chapter One). "Fas-ten-your-seat-belt-and-dial-your-des-ti-na-tion."

"Hi STEV," you say cheerfully. "Ha, ha. This time I'm going to stump you. I've been thinking of where I want to go since Chapter One, and I decided . . ."

The STEV's hum becomes an anxious whine. It wobbles and bounces against the TV antenna on the roof of your house.

"Watch out!" you yell.

"Please-dial-your-des-ti-na-tion," the STEV repeats. Its voice is even creakier.

Loudly and firmly you say, "I want to go to the time of the Messiah." The STEV bounces again, and its viewer screen fills with jagged lightning bolts and exploding stars. Then red lights flash and a message appears on the information panel. "Exact date of messianic era is unknown."

"I know that," you answer, "but you're a Space Time Travel Effectuation Vehicle. You're supposed to reach any time, any place."

A new message appears in large, red letters. "STEV, Inc. takes no responsibility for this irregular trip. If you insist on this destination you must travel at your own risk."

"All right, already! Let's go!" you say.

"To reach Messianic era set time dial to its final, forward setting. Set Locator button to Land of Israel and press Start."

You do it. The humming grows louder. Through the viewer screen you see your house and street and neighborhood dropping away. Quickly you fasten your seat belt. Suddenly you can't see anything. Billowing, black clouds surround the STEV. It begins to buck up and down like a pony at a rodeo. Gusts of wind roar and pound against the sides of the cabin. Then spears of red and orange flames burst through the clouds and sizzle on the viewer screen.

"Yikes!" you yelp. "What's going on?" You push the "Information" button. The answer reads, "Ezekiel, Malachi, and other Bible prophets predicted that a time of war and terrible unrest would come in the future. Later Jewish thinkers believed that the war and unrest would precede the arrival of the Messiah. You are now traveling through that time."

Off to one side a huge, gray-white column rises slowly through the black clouds. The top of the column begins to spread into the deadly shape of a giant mushroom.

"Get me out of here!" you yell and push the red hyper-speed button. With a "va-room" the STEV zooms forward, pushing through the dark, menacing clouds, fighting howling winds, and showers of hail. You clutch the armrests and squeeze your eyes shut.

Finally, the bucking motion slows down. You open your eyes. The clouds have become gray with pink edges. They're growing lighter and lighter. Suddenly the STEV breaks through into a blue, cloudless sky. It lurches out of hyper-speed and begins to float gently.

The red lights flash on the information panel. The message reads, "You have reached your destination. You are cruising eastward over the

Land of Israel during the messianic era. The year is unknown." You take a deep breath and let go of the armrests. Then you look down through the viewer screen at a green, sunny countryside. It's much greener than it was on your first STEV trip, just before the time of Abraham and Sarah.

Little streams twist through rounded hills, splash down in sparkling waterfalls, and flow into blue lakes. Sailboats and canoes move lazily on the lakes. In a meadow near one of the lakes a group of boys and girls are tossing a frisbee. A family has spread a blanket for a picnic nearby. They're singing along with a boy playing guitar.

The STEV sails slowly east and the land begins to rise into higher hills. There's a line of hikers striding along below you, carrying backpacks. They're climbing a trail into the hills. You get worried. The last time you were here, a band of robbers was waiting to attack the people on the trail. Up ahead you see only a deer and a fawn on the trail. They look down at the hikers and then move off into the forest. No robbers.

Of course, how could there be robbers? This is the time of the Messiah. There aren't even any wars. What was it the prophet Isaiah said? You push the "Information" button and punch in "Isaiah" and "Sword." Information reports the prophet's words, "And they (the nations) shall beat their swords into plow blades and their spears into pruning hooks.

Nation shall not lift up sword against nation. Neither shall they learn war anymore."

A girl is sitting on a broad rock looking down into the valley just ahead. Sheep are feeding on the slope of the hill and a mountain lion is sprawled beside her with his head in her lap. "Hey girl, are you crazy?" you yell. "He could take a bite out of you. Run!" But the girl doesn't look up. And as you sail over you notice that there's a lamb cuddled against her leg.

The red light blinks. A new message is being printed on the information panel. "The prophet Isaiah wrote, 'The wolf and the lamb shall feed together and the lion shall eat straw like the ox; . . . they shall not hurt or destroy in all my holy mountain, says the Lord.'"

It's amazing. Everyone is a friend, you think. Of course there must be different ideas about life in these days of the Messiah. My father would want a tennis court nearby. And my mother would want a vegetable garden. I'd want a soccer field and some friends to play ball with. But those are just details. The big picture is the important part—thanking God and living in peace with each other just like the prophets promised in the Bible.

There's something new coming up. "What now?" you wonder. A broad road stretches through the hills. And it's full of people. All kinds and colors of people—black, brown, pink, and tan. Kids are chasing each other through the crowds. Sounds of music float up. There are flutes and clarinets and shrill piccolos. People are singing as they walk. And everyone looks so good. Maybe there are no sick people in the time of the Messiah. Terrific.

Far ahead, all the hills seem to join and rise together into one huge mountain. The top glows in the sunshine. The STEV floats closer over orchards of fruit trees, brooks, ponds, and sweet-smelling gardens. A group of gleaming buildings stand on the mountain. One is topped by a golden dome. A tall tower rises beside another. A third has arches reaching toward the sky.

You feel there's a shimmering presence inside them and floating over them. It makes you tingle with happiness. You're glad to be alive, grateful for the trees and flowers and music around you, grateful for your family and friends. The people standing by the buildings are singing "Hallelujah," praise be to God. Before you can ask, the information panel lights up with the words, "The prophet Micah said, 'In the last days it shall come to pass that the house of the Lord shall be set on top of the

The End (or the Beginning)

mountains. . . . Many nations shall come and say: "Let us go up to the mountain of the Lord and God shall teach us God's ways, and we will walk in God's paths." Torah shall go forth from Zion and the word of the Lord from Jerusalem.'"

Smoothly and noiselessly the STEV begins to float back from the glowing mountain top. It turns and moves down the slope of the mountain.

"Wait a minute," you whisper, "can't we stay a little longer? It's so great here."

A message flashes on the panel, "STEV is allowed only a limited period of time in alternate time zones. We are now returning to our point of origin."

You can't argue with the STEV. You learned that on your last trip. So you close your eyes and try to remember the bright mountain of the Lord, the people and the singing. You didn't see God or the Messiah or the prophet Elijah on the mountain. But you're not disappointed. You felt them inside you. Maybe they are the warm happiness you are still feeling.

But the happiness begins to cool when you remember that the mushroom cloud, the flames, and the roaring wind are still ahead, waiting for you. You'll have to get through them before you reach home. And when you get home you'll find all the old problems. There'll be tests and homework and traffic jams on the way to Grandma's house. You'll still have arguments and fights with your brothers or sisters or the kids at school. You'll still walk past homeless, hungry people on the street. There will still be wars. . . .

The STEV begins to bounce. It's moving into the wind and flames. You hold the armrest tightly, grit your teeth and think about the glowing mountain top. "Some day we have to get there," you say to yourself. "We have to try to live like the Bible teaches us. To remember Isaiah and Amos and the other prophets and make the world a better place. Then some day we'll get to that mountain top."

Bucking and lurching, the STEV struggles through the dark clouds. But flowers, birds, and rippling ribbons of color dance across the viewer screen. Happiness fills you again.

Index